fast
fat need

fast knits
fat needles

SALLY HARDING

**photography by
John Heseltine**

C&T PUBLISHING

Fast Knits Fat Needles

First published in North America
by C&T Publishing, Inc.,
P.O. Box 1456, Lafayette, CA 94549

Copyright © Octopus Publishing Group Ltd. 2005
Illustrations and Photographs © Octopus Publishing Group Ltd. 2005
Knitting designs and text copyright © Sally Harding 2005

ISBN 1-57120-311-7

A CIP record of this book is available from the British Library

Senior Executive Editor Anna Sanderson
Executive Art Editor Auberon Hedgecoe
Project manager Susan Berry
Design Anne Wilson
Illustrations Kate Simunek
Pattern checker Marilyn Wilson
Production Seyhan Esen

Set in Myriad

Color origination by Bright Arts, HK
Printed and bound in China by Toppan Printing Company Ltd.

contents

introduction...

Giant-needle knitting became a passion of mine a couple of years ago when I attended a knitting event in London. Held in the evening in an old Victorian hall, the performance featured knitting songs and poems, and the audience was full of knitting enthusiasts. Young and old, experts and absolute beginners packed the hall. Audience participation was part of the event—those of us who knit were expected to teach novices how to get going with the yarn and needles that were provided free. Because seasoned knitters were told to come with their knitting, I had brought the biggest needles in my cupboard—bright blue 15mm (US size 19) ones. They seemed perfect for celebrating the craft! Giant needles weren't seen around as often then, so many people commented with astonishment on my needles and the huge knitted loops they formed.

This scintillating knitting get-together and the wide eyes of new knitters when they saw the fat needles, sparked off my desire to experiment with giant needles. Knitting with giant needles is surely the most fun thing you can do with knitting. The textures created are exciting and versatile, and they form so quickly that your knitting is finished in a flash—perfect for hectic modern lifestyles and for making last-minute gifts for loved ones.

My growing enthusiasm made me want to share the enjoyment of giant-needle knitting with as many people as I could; hence this book full of tips and techniques, and the simplest of projects—a book for knitters of every skill level, as well as absolute beginners.

The designs in this collection would all be considered "easy" knits. Many of them are actually super-easy and most of the scarves fall into this category. There is only one item that is shaped—the handbag on page 72—everything else is made of either squares or rectangles. Some designs give tasters of various easy knitting techniques—very simple pattern stitches or very simple colorwork. Although each design is easy to make on its own, if you had never knit before and actually made everything in the book you would have covered a wide range of knitting techniques and learned a great deal about knitting.

There are no sweaters in the book because I wanted this to be a book that absolute beginners could pick up and have fun with. Designs that they could finish quickly and add tantalizing trims to. Knitting accessories and home furnishing items eliminates the worry of wondering whether your finished knitting will "fit" you or a recipient in the right way, not a small worry when you're starting out. Sweaters are best left until all the techniques have been mastered and the process of knitting is a true pleasure.

If you're a seasoned knitter and think the giant textures are too unsophisticated, have a go with some of your favorite yarns or with fabric strips and see what you think—you may find yourself a convert. The speed of it all is so very tempting. And working giant-needle knits is the perfect light relief from complicated sweaters in fine yarns.

To absolute beginners, I say that learning to knit with big needles will be a really enjoyable experience. You can learn to knit and make a scarf all in the same day! Then, like the rest of us knitters, you'll be hooked for life!

—Sally Harding

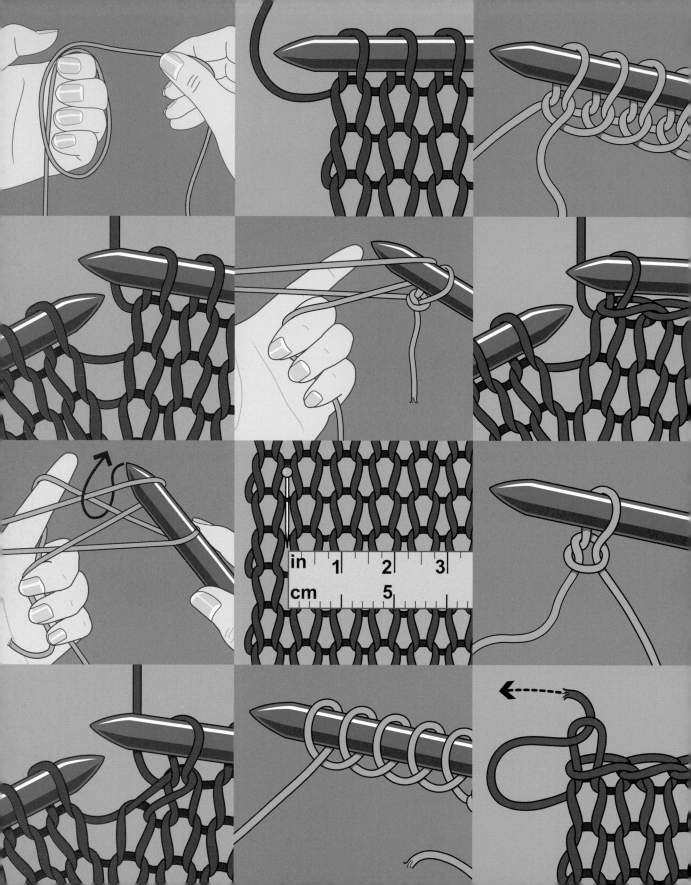

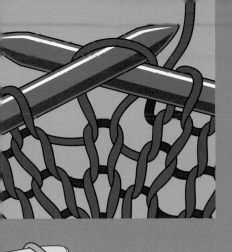

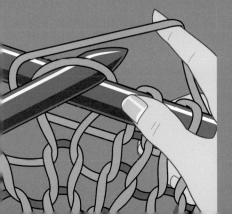

giant-
needle
know-
how

knitting basics...

Learning to knit using giant needles is a lot more fun than learning to knit with standard-size needles. You can really see what is going on with the loops and your knitting grows surprisingly fast. This chapter provides all the basic know-how needed for simple knitting techniques, from casting on your stitches to fastening them off.

Absolute beginners can follow the step-by-step instructions to learn all the techniques they need to know to get started, and knitters who haven't picked up their needles for years can use the illustrations as a refresher course. There are tips for working with fat needles throughout this chapter.

Before embarking on the techniques or on any of the projects in the book, read about all the different "yarns" you can use for your giant-needle knitting and take a look at the exciting textures they produce.

yarns for giant needles

Don't be fooled by giant needles. They aren't only for really thick yarns. You can use them to knit any yarn—you could knit sewing thread with them, in fact. Thin yarns will form airy, draping textures when worked on giant needles, and fat yarns will form firm knits. You can create your own thicknesses of yarns by working with several strands held together. These strands can be all of the same yarn or a mixture of yarns with varying textures.

One of my favorite yarns for giant needles is "rag" yarn—strips of cut or torn fabric from 1/2 inch to 3 inches (12mm to 9cm) wide. Turn to pages 12–15 to see some sample textures.

choosing giant needles

To me, giant (or "fat") needles range from 10mm (US size 15) through 25mm (US size 50). I have chosen to start the "giant" size range with 10mm because many years ago they were considered the very fattest knitting needles around. The majority of the designs in this book are worked on 15mm

(US size 19), most of the others are worked either on 12mm (US size 17) or 20mm (US size 35), and one is worked on super-giant 25mm (US size 50). My 25mm-needle design is the Scrap Scarf on page 40—it begs to be made into your very own original.

To try out giant-needle knitting, I recommend that you buy 12mm (US size 17) and 15mm (US size 19) needles. Look for colored ones. They're so much more cheerful than those boring gray ones. If you find holding a pair of huge needles awkward, try a giant circular needle—two knitting points joined by a plastic cord. They do away with bulky knitting-needle ends, so are lighter, more manageable, and easy to carry around.

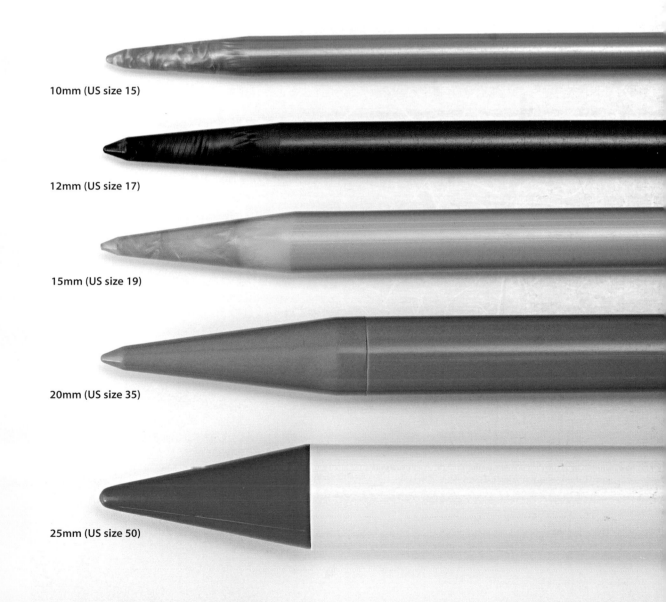

10mm (US size 15)

12mm (US size 17)

15mm (US size 19)

20mm (US size 35)

25mm (US size 50)

giant-needle textures

Here are some examples of giant-needle textures to whet your appetite. Hopefully they will inspire you to try out all sorts of yarns with your fat needles. Giant loops show off the qualities of a yarn so beautifully. Try using just one strand of a particular yarn, or mix several strands together and knit with them as one, or change the yarn type every row or every other row (see Scrap Scarves on page 36).

The loosest textures are good for anything that can drape, like scarves, wraps, and string bags. The firmer textures suit cushion covers, throws, and drawstring bags. And the really firm textures are ideal for rugs and strong bags.

Opposite: Cotton yarn and mohair yarn worked on 12mm (US size 17) knitting needles.

Below: A tape yarn and a superthick wool yarn worked on 25mm (US size 50) knitting needles.

Above: Chenille, tape, silk, and fabric-strip yarns worked on 15mm (US size 19) knitting needles.

Above: "Rag" knitting worked with fabric strips on 15mm (US size 19) needles.

casting on your stitches...

"Casting on" is the first thing you do when starting a piece of knitting to create the first loops, or "stitches," on your needle. There are many, many ways to cast on, but only the ones called for in the instructions in this book are given here—the single cast-on and the double cast-on. Where no specific cast-on method is mentioned in the instructions you can use any method you're comfortable with.

To practice casting on for the first time, use 12mm (US size 17) knitting needles and a thick wool yarn. Form about 14 loops on your needle and knit two rows (see following pages). Then discard these stitches or unravel them and start over. Repeat this process several times until your cast-on loops are just tight enough to hug the needle but not too tight to work the first row comfortably. In giant-needle knitting it is especially important not to cast on too tightly. Once you can cast on without thinking about it you've cracked it and nothing else in knitting will be as hard to learn. If you find it easy, you're a natural!

making the first loop

For most cast-ons, start by forming a slip knot (also called a slip loop) on the knitting needle. This is a simple knot that is secure but still allows the loop on the needle to expand. The steps here show the "tail" end of the knot quite short; this is only to make clear which is the tail end and which the ball end of the yarn. In fact, you should leave a long tail of yarn to weave into the finished knitting—at least 6 inches (15cm).

1 Lay the yarn over the fingers of one hand, with the tail end hanging in the center of your palm. Then wrap the yarn once around your fingers to form a circle.

2 Insert a knitting needle through the circle of yarn from front to back and draw the ball end of the yarn through the circle (as shown by the arrow) to form a loop on the needle.

3 Pull both ends of the yarn to tighten the new loop on the knitting needle, but leave it just loose enough to move freely along the needle. You have now made your first stitch.

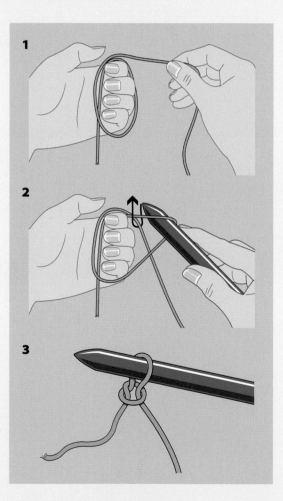

simple cast-ons

Try both the single cast-on method given below and the double cast-on method shown on the next page. The single cast-on is sometimes called the "thumb method." It is probably the easiest cast-on to learn and is often used to cast on several stitches onto the end of a row in the middle of your knitting (see the boas on page 46). You can also use it to add a single stitch at the end of a row or to replace stitches that were bound/cast off in the previous row for a buttonhole (see Button Cushion on page 104).

The double cast-on is my favorite method and was passed down to me by my grandmother. It makes the first row of knitting easier to work and it forms a nice firm edge.

You can start the double cast-on with a slip knot on the needle or without one. I tend to omit the slip knot in a rush to get those loops on the needle.

Single cast-on

1 Make a slip knot on your knitting needle and hold the needle in your right hand. Hold the yarn in your left hand and loop it around your thumb as shown. Insert the tip of the needle under and through the front of this loop as shown by the arrow.

2 Once the new loop of yarn is on the needle, release your thumb from the loop and at the same time pull the yarn to tighten it around the needle.

3 Slip your left thumb under the yarn to again form a loop around it (see Step 1) and continue casting on loops in the same way. The loops should be tight enough to hug the needle but loose enough to slide easily along it.

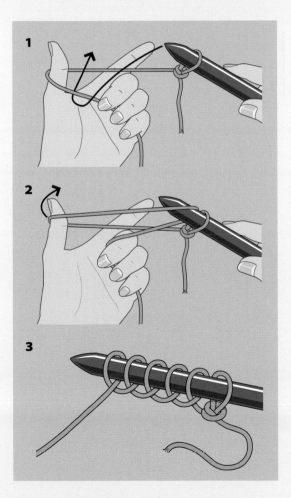

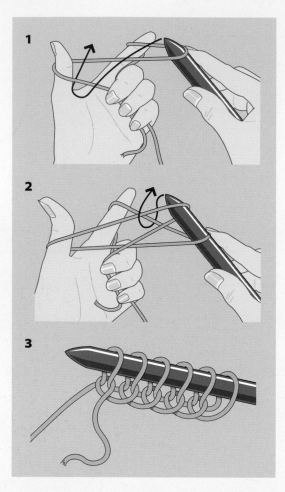

Double cast-on

1 Make a slip knot on your needle or simply wrap the yarn over the top of the needle as shown, so that you have a very long tail end at the front of the needle. Hold the yarn in your left hand with the tail end around your thumb and the ball end around your index finger. Then insert the needle under the front of the loop on your thumb as shown by the arrow.

2 With the tip of the needle, draw the ball end of the yarn (held by your left index finger) through the new loop on the needle as shown by the arrow, then release the loop around the thumb.

3 Pull the yarn ends to tighten the loop on the needle. Reinsert the thumb under the tail end of the yarn and make the next loop in the same way. Continue until you have as many loops as you need.

holding yarn and needles...

If you already know how to knit, you will have your own particular way of holding your yarn and needles and you should stick to it. Knitting style is a matter of preference, and of comfort and ease. If you are a beginner, try out the two ways of holding the yarn and see which one you find easiest. All knitting

stitches and instructions are exactly the same whichever style you choose.

"English" knitting is a style that British knitters have passed down over generations and have generally stuck with. The only way in which it differs from "Continental" knitting is that the yarn is held in the right hand and fed into the knitting with the index finger. In Continental-style knitting, the yarn is usually held in the left hand. You can probably knit faster with the Continental-style knitting method, but your criteria for choosing one style over the other should be ease and comfort rather than speed, and that will be determined by your personal dexterity. (Left-handed knitters will need to reverse the instructions given here.)

english-style knitting

Holding the yarn: The yarn is laced through the fingers of the right hand and over the index finger. The aim is to tension the yarn while letting it slip through the fingers. As you learn to knit, try lacing the yarn over and under the fingers of the right hand in different ways if this one doesn't work for you.

Holding the needles: The knitting is worked with one needle in each hand. Each new stitch is formed by wrapping the yarn around the tip of the right-hand needle—sometimes called "throwing" the yarn. The index finger is brought forward to pass the yarn around the needle tip.

continental-style knitting

Holding the yarn: For this style of knitting, the yarn is laced through the fingers of the left hand and over the index finger. This is just an example of how to lace the yarn. Try whatever way helps you to tension the yarn and at the same time lets the yarn slip through your fingers as you use it to form new loops.

Holding the needles: In Continental-style knitting the needles are held as for English-style knitting. However, instead of "throwing" the yarn around the right-hand needle, your index finger positions the yarn so that you can catch it with the tip of the right-hand needle and draw it through the loop. In other words, you "grab" the yarn with the right-hand needle as you would with a crochet hook.

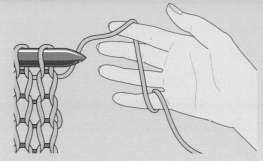

Holding the yarn

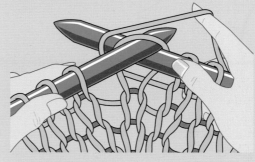

Holding the needles

CONTINENTAL-STYLE KNITTING

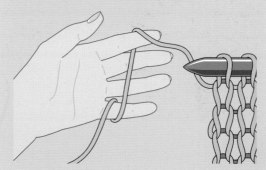

Holding the yarn

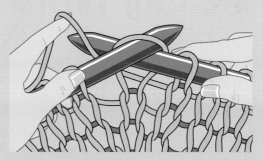

Holding the needles

learning the knit stitch...

There are only two stitches to learn in knitting—the knit stitch and the purl stitch. All knitting textures, from the simplest to the most complex, are formed with combinations of knit and purl stitches.

Absolute beginners can follow the steps here to learn the knit and purl stitches, and knitters who haven't picked up their needles for a while can use them to refresh their memory.

Casting on and knitting the very first row is probably the hardest thing to learn in knitting. If you are an absolute beginner and want to learn the basics from scratch, it will help to find a knitter to cast on for you and knit a few rows. Then try out the knit stitch until you get the hang of it—it's really easy! Once you're hooked on the fun of seeing the textile grow under your fingers, you'll have a pressing reason to learn to cast on.

how to knit a stitch

To practice or learn the knit stitch, first cast on about 14 stitches (see pages 16–18). Then hold the needle with the loops on it in your left hand and the empty needle in your right hand. Lace the yarn through your fingers (as explained on page 19). For clarity, the illustrations show a row being worked in the middle of your knitting, but the principle is just the same if you are starting with the first cast-on loops.

1 With the yarn behind your knitting, insert the right-hand needle from front to back through the center of the first stitch on the left-hand needle.

2 Next, wrap the yarn around the tip of the right-hand needle. Draw the yarn through the loop on the left-hand needle (as shown by the arrow) to form a new loop on the right-hand needle.

3 Drop the loop (that you just worked through) off the left-hand needle. You have knit one stitch—called "knit one" or "k1" in knitting parlance (see page 127 for a list of the main abbreviations used in knitting patterns). Knit all the stitches remaining on the left-hand needle and you will have completed "one knit row."

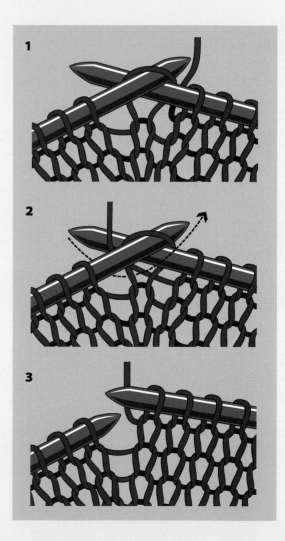

learning the purl stitch...

The purl stitch may take a little more time to learn than the knit stitch, so try to master the knit stitch first. After completing one row of knitting, transfer the needle with the loops on it to your left hand and the empty needle to your right hand. Keep working knit rows until you get the hang of it. The fabric that results from knitting every row is called garter stitch (see page 23). Make sure your loops aren't too tight on your giant needles and don't worry if your knitting isn't perfectly smooth. An even, smooth fabric will develop slowly with more practice.

Once you can work the purl stitch as well as the knit stitch, you will be able to form an enormous number of knitting textures. The three main knitting textures are shown on page 23—garter stitch, stockinette/stocking stitch, and reverse stockinette/stocking stitch.

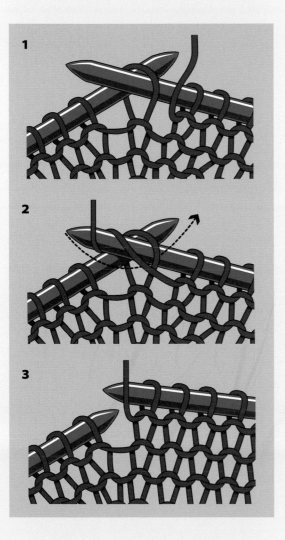

how to purl a stitch

If you are trying the purl stitch for the first time, cast on and work several rows in knit stitch so you have some knitting to hold on to below the needles. Hold the needle with all the stitches in your left hand and the empty needle in your right hand ready to start the next row. By now you should have found the method of holding your yarn that suits you best and is second nature, so you no longer have to think about it.

1 With the yarn at the front, insert the right-hand needle from right to left through the center of the first stitch on the left-hand needle.

2 Next, wrap the yarn around the tip of the right-hand needle. Draw the yarn through the loop on the left-hand needle (as shown by the arrow) to form a new loop on the right-hand needle.

3 Then drop the loop (that you just worked through) off the left-hand needle. You have just purled one stitch—called "purl one" or "p1" in knitting parlance. Purl all the stitches remaining on the left-hand needle and you will have completed "one purl row."

add or subtract stitches...

Increases (added stitches) and decreases (subtracted stitches) are used to shape your knitting. They also play a part in the creation of a vast variety of knitting textures. Although there are many things you can knit just using the knit and purl stitches, you need to learn to increase and decrease stitches to go from a beginner knitter to an intermediate knitter.

One very simple increase and one very simple decrease are shown here for you to learn. They are the simple techniques employed to shape the handbag on page 72 and are the most common of all the techniques for increasing and decreasing. Simple sweater shapes are within your reach once you master these.

simple increase

1 On a knit row, insert the needle in the next stitch and knit it—but instead of slipping it off the left-hand needle leave it there and insert the needle into the back of the same stitch and knit it again.

2 You have now knit twice into the stitch on the left-hand needle and can drop it off the needle. There is now one extra stitch in the row. This is called "increase one" (inc 1) or "make one" (m1).

simple decrease

1 On a knit row, insert the right-hand needle first through the second stitch on the left-hand needle, then the first. Draw a loop through in the usual way.

2 Next, drop the two old stitches off the left-hand needle. There is now one less stitch in the row. This is called "knit two together" (k2tog). This decrease can also be used when the knitting pattern says "decrease one" (dec 1).

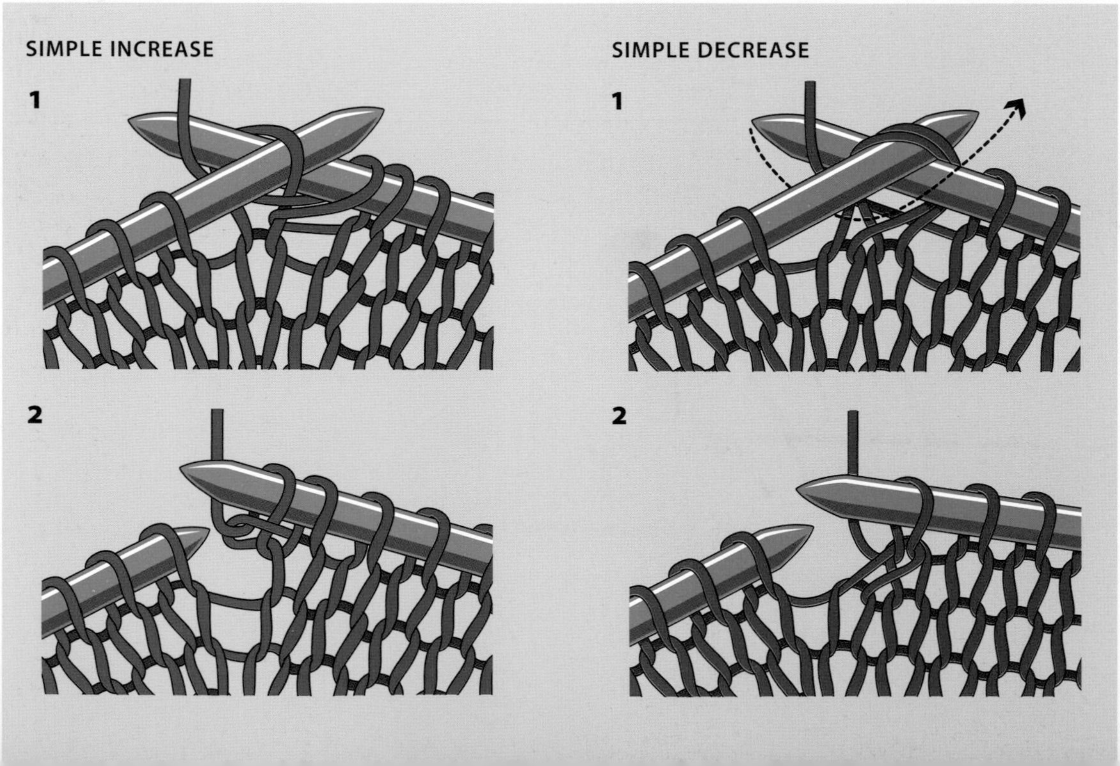

SIMPLE INCREASE

1

2

SIMPLE DECREASE

1

2

simple stitches...

GARTER STITCH

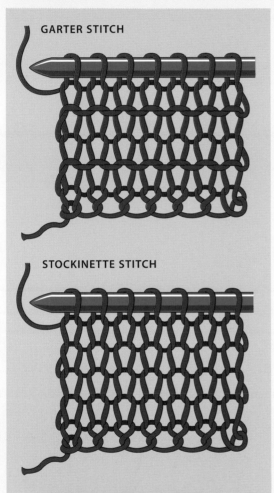

STOCKINETTE STITCH

REVERSE STOCKINETTE STITCH

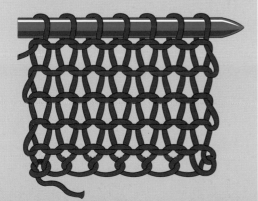

The simplest and most commonly used knitting stitches are garter stitch, stockinette stitch (also called stocking stitch), and reverse stockinette stitch (also called reverse stocking stitch). The illustrations on the left show exactly how the loops are formed.

garter stitch

This texture is especially attractive when knit with fat needles. To form garter stitch, you knit every row. Because the back of a knit stitch is actually a purl stitch and the back of a purl stitch a knit stitch, garter stitch is also formed if you purl every row. Purling is a little slower than knitting, so most people prefer to create garter stitch with knit stitches. Many of the simplest projects in this book use only garter stitch.

stockinette/stocking stitch

Stockinette/stocking stitch forms the smooth texture that is probably most easily recognized as knitting. To form stockinette/stocking stitch, you knit one row and purl one row alternately. The smooth knit side of the stitch is the right side of the knitted fabric and the knobbly purl side the wrong side. (See the Drawstring Knapsack pictured on page 77 for a good example of the stockinette/stocking stitch texture.)

reverse stockinette/stocking stitch

This stitch is worked in exactly the same way as stockinette/stocking stitch. The difference is that in reverse stockinette/stocking stitch the front of the knitted fabric is the knobbly purl side, while the smooth knit side is the wrong side.

fastening off the stitches...

Fastening off your knitting once it is complete is known as "binding off" or "casting off" the stitches. It is done as you work across the row, either knitting or purling as the instructions indicate. "Bind/cast off knitwise" means that you should knit the row as you fasten off the stitches, and "bind/cast off purlwise" means you should purl the stitches as you fasten off. The knitwise version is shown here, but the principle is just the same for the purlwise technique.

Take special care when binding/casting off with giant needles—smooth edges can be tricky to achieve using giant needles since the inconsistencies are so obvious. Cast/bind off slowly and don't pull the yarn too tightly. If the bound-/cast-off edge ends up either very uneven or too tight or too loose, have the patience to try again. The second attempt is sure to put it right. And as you're working with fat needles, even a couple of attempts will only take a few minutes of effort.

how to bind/cast off

1 Knit the first two stitches off the left-hand needle, so there are two stitches on the right-hand needle. Insert the tip of the left-hand needle through the first stitch on the right-hand needle and lift it up and over the second stitch and off the right-hand needle as shown by the arrow.

2 Now that the first stitch has been bound/cast off, there is only one stitch left on the right-hand needle. Knit the next stitch on the left-hand needle so you have two stitches on the right-hand needle again. Again insert the tip of the left-hand needle through the first stitch on the right-hand needle and lift it up and over the second stitch and off the right-hand needle. Continue in this way across all the stitches.

3 When all the stitches have been bound/cast off the left-hand needle, one stitch will still remain on the right-hand needle. To fasten off this last stitch, cut the yarn, leaving a loose end for weaving in later, and thread this end through the last stitch. Pull the end to tighten the loop.

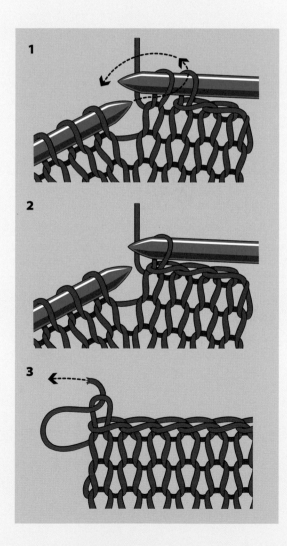

following a pattern...

Once you have grasped the basics, you'll be ready to follow a knitting pattern. Knitting patterns generally follow the same format. They start by giving the size of the finished item. Following this is a list of yarn, needles, and any other materials you'll need. Next comes the recommended gauge/tension (see below) and any special tips you need to read before casting on your stitches.

knitting abbreviations

The row-by-row instructions in a knitting pattern make use of abbreviations. These abbreviations save on space and make the directions easier and quicker to follow. Don't let yourself be put off by knitting terminology and abbreviations—they are logical and extremely easy to learn. For example, "p1" means purl one stitch and "k1" means knit one stitch. All the knitting abbreviations used in this book are given at the back for easy reference (see page 127). They include all those most commonly used in knitting shorthand.

tip boxes in the patterns

Tip boxes and special how-to boxes are sprinkled throughout the instructions for the giant-needle knits. Be sure to make use of these—they are the next best thing to having an experienced knitter at your elbow guiding you through a project. The Before You Start section at the beginning of each pattern also has many useful tips.

gauge/tension...

Some people knit really tightly, some loosely, and others neither particularly tightly nor loosely. There is no right or wrong tightness. It just means that knitters who use the same needle size and yarn and cast on the same number of stitches will produce a piece of knitting that is similar in size but not exactly the same. Your knitting pattern will tell you the size of stitch you should aim for— this is called the "gauge" or "tension." It indicates how many stitches and rows there should be over 4 inches (10cm) of knitting. Before you begin a project it is usually a good idea to test your gauge/tension by making a swatch of knitting and measuring the number of stitches and rows to 4 inches (10cm). You can then, if necessary, use a different needle size to increase or decrease the

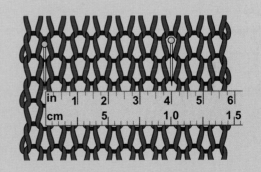

size of the stitches. If you are a beginner working with fat needles, don't worry too much about your stitch size. It won't become that important until you are knitting carefully fitted garments worked in small stitches. Experienced knitters who normally knit tightly will find that giant-needle loops are easier to work if they knit slightly looser.

projects

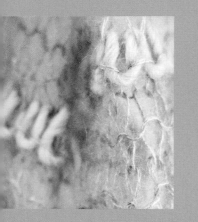

gossamer scarf

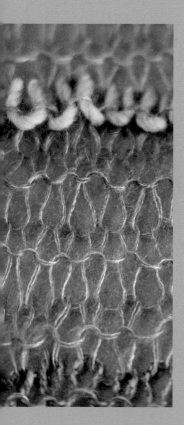

The main yarn used for this wispy scarf is a very fine mohair mix. There's no special stitch needed to create the lacy effect—simple garter stitch, fine yarn, and giant needles do the trick. Strands of differently textured yarns add striking stripe details. Because the scarf folds up into practically nothing and it is really light, it's great for packing up when traveling. Tie the ends of the scarf into loose knots for a smart look or to make it shorter (see page 31). For an evening scarf, you could knit it with just one color of mohair and dress up the finished knitting by stitching on a few subtle sprinkles of sequins.

here's how...

When knitting this scarf, you'll find that the loops of mohair will slide more easily along the needles if you keep the knitting fairly loose. If you use a slightly thicker mohair, you will need to use only one strand instead of two strands together.

how big is it?

When hanging, the finished scarf measures approximately 12in/30cm wide x 63in/160cm long.

which stitches?

Garter stitch

how much yarn?

MC = fine mohair yarn in main color
2 x 1oz/25g balls Rowan *Kid Silk Haze* (blue—shade no. 592—or chosen color)

A = fine mohair yarn in first contrasting color
1 x ball Rowan *Kid Silk Haze* (olive—shade no. 597—or chosen color)

B = fine mohair yarn in second contrasting color
1 x ball Rowan *Kid Silk Haze* (khaki—shade no. 601—or chosen color)

C = olive chunky yarn in third contrasting color
small amount Rowan *Polar* (olive—shade no. 642—or chosen color)

D = chunky chenille yarn in fourth contrasting color
small amount Rowan *Chunky Cotton Chenille* (sea blue—shade no. 392—or chosen color)

E = lightweight silk and cotton blend yarn in fifth contrasting color
small amount Rowan *Summer Tweed* (turquoise—shade no. 512—or chosen color)

(*See page 124 for yarn tips*)

which needles?

Pair of 15mm (US size 19) knitting needles

what gauge/tension?

$6^1/_2$ sts to 4in/10cm measured over garter st (and lying flat) using two strands MC held tog and 15mm (US size 19) needles.

before you start

- There is no need to check your gauge/tension before beginning as an exact size is not essential for a scarf. (If you want to know more about gauge/tension, turn to page 25.)
- *For knitting abbreviations, turn to page 127.*

cast on

Using 15mm (US size 19) needles and two strands MC held tog, cast on 24 sts loosely.
Using two strands of mohair yarn and one strand of other yarns throughout, work in garter st (k every row) in a random stripe patt *or* in stripe patt as foll:
*8 rows MC, 1 row C, 5 rows A, 4 rows B, and 2 rows A. **
10 rows MC, 1 row D, 3 rows MC, 1 row C, 3 rows A, 4 rows MC, 1 row E, and 5 rows MC.***
Rep from * to *** once more, then rep from * to ** once.
Knit 3 rows MC, 1 row D, 3 rows MC.

try this!

You only need a small amount of yarns C, D, and E, so instead of buying a whole ball of each yarn, use your own scraps in sympathetic shades, or choose the main color and yarns A and B to go with your own scraps.

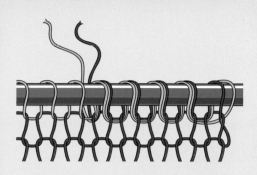

knit in the loose ends!

The mohair yarn is so fine that you can "knit in" the loose ends at the beginning and end of the mohair stripes. Just knit the first stitch of the row with the new yarn and the end of the old yarn, then knit the next four or five stitches with the new yarn and the ends of the old and new yarn held together. Trim off the yarn ends close to the knitting when the work is completed.

bind/cast off

Bind/cast off all 24 sts knitwise.

finishing touches

Weave in any loose ends. Split the end of thick yarn in half and weave in each half separately.

alternative colorways

For an original creation, make your own selection of colors for your Gossamer Scarf. The super-delicate scarves above and below were knit with just a single strand of mohair, and knots were tied through a stripe near the ends for a smart detail.

Made with a superthick variegated wool yarn on very fat needles, this scarf is also really easy. It is knit back and forth from end to end rather than side to side—the usual way of knitting a scarf. Just cast on and eight rows later it's finished! No need to add the fringe later since the random-length fringe is a "self-fringe" integrated into the

ridged scarf with fringe

knitting—each row uses a fresh piece of yarn left hanging at the beginning and end for a fringe. This scarf could be made into a more masculine-looking accessory by omitting the fringed ends and just knitting the ridged texture in a more subdued palette. To make it for a child, shorten the length and width by a few stitches and rows.

here's how...

This scarf is so quick that you could easily knit several and give them as gifts. Handmade scarves are always treasured by the recipient, never go out of fashion, and will keep a much-loved friend or family member warm for many winters.

how big is it?
Lying flat, the finished scarf measures approximately 4³/₄in/12cm wide x 43¹/₂in/109cm long, excluding the fringe. When hanging around the neck, it stretches to about 51in/130cm long.

which stitches?
- Stockinette/stocking stitch (St st)
- Reverse stockinette/stocking stitch

how much yarn?
Superchunky yarn—
2 x 3¹/₂oz/100g balls Rowan *Biggy Print*
   (shade no. 255 or chosen color)
(*See page 124 for yarn tips*)

try this!
- If you find the stitches are getting loose at the edges of the scarf, knot the ends together very loosely as the work progresses and readjust to make a neater knotted fringe when the scarf is finished.

- The stitches of this scarf fit on a pair of needles 14 inches (35cm) long, but for a longer scarf you'd need to use a circular needle, which holds many more stitches.

which needles?
Pair of 20mm (US size 35) knitting needles

what gauge/tension?
5¹/₂ sts and 7 rows to 4in/10cm measured over St st using 20mm (US size 35) needles.

before you start
- There is no need to check your gauge/tension before beginning as an exact size is not essential for a scarf.
- If you want to use a different yarn for this scarf, make a gauge/tension swatch with it to figure out how many stitches to cast on for the entire length of the scarf. Use two or three strands of yarn held together if your chosen yarn is not a superchunky weight.
- See the Try This tip box (below left) for the type of knitting needles to use for a scarf longer than the one shown here (which is 43¹/₂in/109cm long).
- Remember to work each row of the scarf with a new length of yarn, leaving a long loose end at the beginning and end of each row. These ends form the fringe. Vary the end lengths between 7³/₄–14¹/₂in/20–37cm for a random-length fringe.
- *For knitting abbreviations, turn to page 127.*

cast on
First, cut two lengths of yarn—one 4¹/₂yd/4m long and one 6yd/5.5m long. Tie lengths tog at one end, positioning knot 12in/30cm from cut ends. Place knot on top of a 20mm (US size 35) needle, with shorter length at front of needle and longer one at back of needle, and use the long lengths to cast on 60 sts loosely using the double cast-on method (see page 18). This will create two strands of fringe at the beg and end of the cast-on row.

Using 20mm (US size 35) needles, starting a new length of yarn for each row, and leaving a long loose end at each end, work 8 rows of the scarf as foll:
K one row.
P one row.
[K 2 rows, p one row] twice.

bind/cast off
Again starting a new length of yarn, bind/cast off all 60 sts loosely knitwise.

finishing touches
At each end of the scarf, knot the loose ends of yarn together close to the scarf edge—start at the cast-on edge and tie the first eight loose ends together in pairs, then tie the last three strands together. Make sure the strands of the fringe are random lengths and tie a knot near the end of each one. Trim the ends close to the end knots.

alternative colorway
The scarf above was worked in exactly the same way as the one pictured on page 32, but with a different shade of Rowan *Biggy Print*. The tight and loose twists of this variegated yarn create a great texture for a fun fringe.

scrap scarves

The simple instructions for these striped scarves will inspire you to knit creations of your own. Use your own leftovers or collect scraps of yarns from friends. For a harmonious design, limit the palette to just a few colors, but use as many different textures as you can. Cozy winter scarves need some warm wools, but decorative scarves are best worked in cottons—bouclés, knitting tapes, rag strips, and a mixture of thick and thin knitting yarns. Because the scarves are narrow, they look good as short scarves, too.

here's how...

There are two scrap scarf patterns to choose from. The Horizontal-stripe Scarf (see opposite and page 37) is worked from side to side in the usual way, but the Vertical-stripe Scarf (see page 40) is knit from end to end in only nine rows and needs a circular needle to accommodate all the stitches.

how big is it?
- **Horizontal-stripe scarf:** The finished scarf measures approximately 4½in/11cm wide x 71in/180cm long.
- **Vertical-stripe scarf:** When hanging, the finished scarf measures approximately 4½in/11cm wide x 79½in/202cm long.

which stitches?
Garter stitch

how much yarn?
Small amount of each yarn as foll:

Horizontal-stripe scarf

A = duck-egg blue cotton tape yarn—use two strands held tog

B = pale mauve chunky wool yarn—use two strands held tog

C = mauve silk and cotton blend yarn—use two strands held tog

D = mauve lightweight metallic yarn—use two strands held tog

E = olive-toned superchunky yarn—use one strand

F = olive cotton tape yarn—use two strands held tog

G = duck-egg blue lightweight fabric (⅓yd/30cm of 44in/112cm wide fabric)—cut into ¾in/2cm wide strips

Vertical-stripe scarf

A = duck-egg blue lightweight cotton bouclé yarn—use two strands held tog

B = pale mauve chunky wool yarn—use two strands held tog

C = mauve silk and cotton blend yarn—use two strands held tog

D = gray-green cotton tape yarn—use two strands held tog

E = olive-toned superchunky yarn—use one strand

(*See Before You Start below and page 124 for yarn tips*)

which needles?
- **Horizontal-stripe scarf:** pair of 25mm (US size 50) knitting needles
- **Vertical-stripe scarf:** long 20mm (US size 35) circular knitting needle

what gauge/tension?
- **Horizontal-stripe scarf:** Approximately 8 sts to 4in/10cm measured over garter st using 25mm (US size 50) needles.
- **Vertical-stripe scarf:** Approximately 4 sts to 4in/10cm measured over garter st using 20mm (US size 35) needles.

before you start
- Choose the yarns you are going to use first. The yarns listed are just an example of what you can use. Try to pick four or five different textures and use the thinner yarns double. The Vertical-stripe Scarf shown used Rowan *Polar* (shade no. 650) for the chunky wool (B), Rowan *Summer Tweed* (shade no. 501) for the silk and cotton blend (C), and Rowan *Biggy Print* (shade no. 245) for the superchunky yarn (E). The Horizontal-stripe Scarf shown used the same Rowan yarns for B, C, and E, plus Rowan *Lurex Shimmer* for the metallic yarn (D). Leftover tape yarns and bouclé were used for the other colors.

- Be sure to use a cotton yarn for A, so that the cast-on and bound-/cast-off edges are firm and not too stretchy.
- There is no need to check your gauge/tension before beginning as an exact size is not essential for scarves and the knitting is very stretchy.
- *For knitting abbreviations, turn to page 127.*

horizontal-stripe scarf

cast on

First, cut at least 12 strips of fabric, ³/₄in/2cm wide (see pages 60 and 95 for how to prepare "rag" knitting strips).

Using 25mm (US size 50) needles and A, cast on 9 sts using the single cast-on method (see page 17). Starting a new length of yarn for each row, leaving long ends for the fringe, and knotting the new yarn onto the old before beg the row, work in garter st (k every row) in random stripes or in the following stripe sequence:

*1 row A.
1 row B.
1 row C and D (used tog).
1 row F.
1 row E.
1 row G.*
Rep from * to *, until scarf measures, when hanging, 71in/180cm from cast-on edge or desired length.

bind/cast off

Using A, bind/cast off all 9 sts knitwise.

finishing touches

Trim the fringe of yarn ends to 1¹/₂in/4cm from the knots.

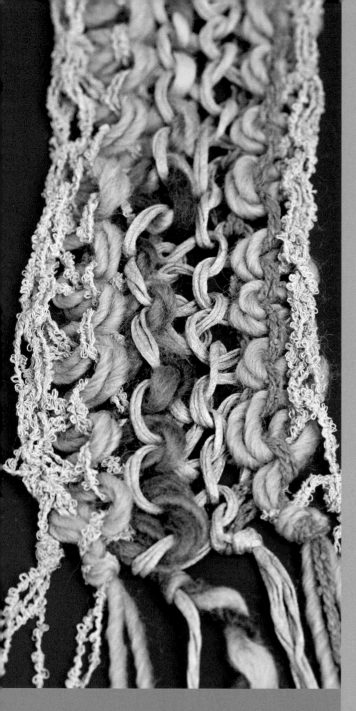

vertical-stripe scarf

cast on

First, cut two lengths of A (used double)—one 5½ yd/5m long and one 7yd/6.5m long. Tie lengths tog at one end, positioning knot 10in/25cm from the cut ends.

Place knot on top of a 20mm (US size 35) circular needle, with shorter strand at front of needle and longer one at back of needle, and use the long lengths to cast on 78 sts loosely with the double cast-on method (see page 18). This will create two strands of fringe at the beg and end of the cast-on row.

Starting a new length of yarn for each row and leaving long loose ends for fringe at each end, work garter st (k every row) back and forth on the circular needle in random stripes or in the foll stripe sequence:

1 row B.
1 row C.
3 rows D.
1 row E.
1 row A.
1 row B.
1 row A.

bind/cast off

Using A, bind/cast off all 78 sts very loosely knitwise. (Try to match firmness/looseness of this edge to cast-on edge.)

finishing touches

At each end of the scarf, knot the loose ends of yarn together in pairs close to the scarf edge. Trim the fringe to 2¼in/6cm from the knots.

vertical-stripe scarf

All the stitches for the entire length of the Vertical-stripe Scarf (above and right) are cast on at the beginning. After only nine rows the scarf is complete. The yarn ends at each end of each row form the "self-fringe."

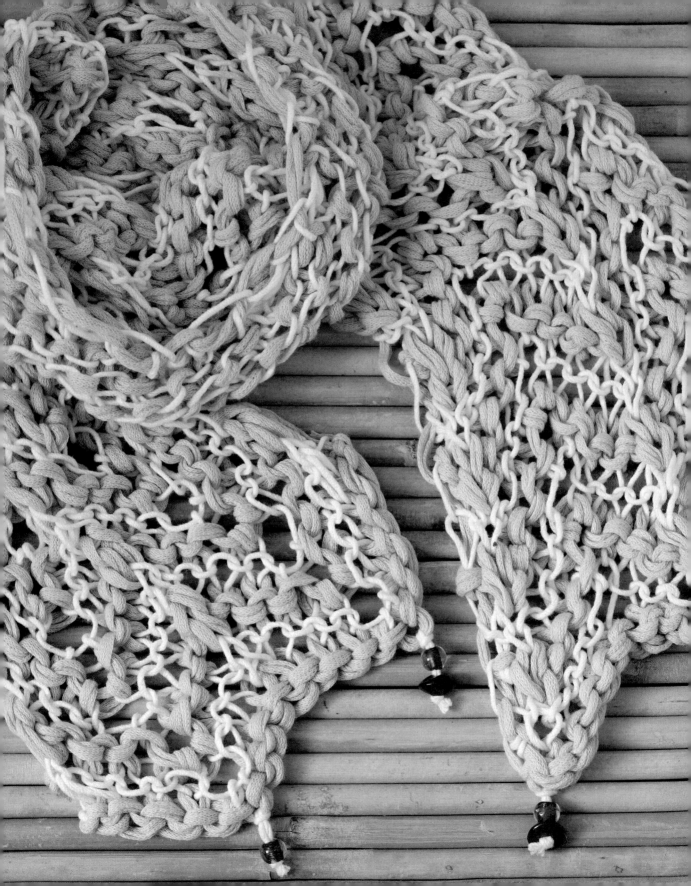

Once you have mastered the basic stitches, you will discover how enjoyable it is to knit pattern stitches. Simple manipulation of the loops can create the most delectable textures, which form magically beneath the needles. The zigzag pattern used for this cotton scarf is a traditional stitch employed for knitted afghans. Although there is usually a "right" side of this fabric and a "wrong" one, in this giant-needle rendition both sides look great. Beginners who have practiced simple garter stitch should try knitting this scarf as an introduction to the increasing and decreasing techniques used to create the lacy pattern. It makes good preparation before moving on to more complicated lace stitches.

zigzag scarf

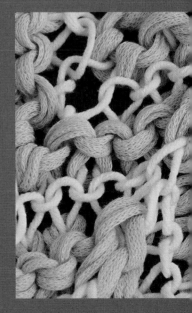

here's how...

The simple "yarn over" increases used in the zigzag pattern form even bigger holes than the fat needles do already. Instructions for making the yarn overs are integrated into the instructions.

how big is it?
When hanging, the finished scarf measures approximately 7in/18cm wide x 67in/170cm long.

which stitches?
A traditional zigzag afghan stitch

how much yarn?
A = cotton tape yarn in first color
   3 x 1¾oz/50g balls Rowan *Cotton Tape* (beige—shade no. 542—or chosen color) or Rowan *Linen Tape* in desired shade
B = medium-weight cotton yarn in second color
   1 x 1¾oz/50g ball Rowan *All Seasons Cotton* (white—shade no. 178—or chosen color)
(*See page 124 for yarn tips*)

which needles?
Pair of 15mm (US size 19) knitting needles

any extras?
- 5 round glass beads, 11mm in diameter
- 5 flattish round beads, 17mm in diameter

what gauge/tension?
12½ sts and 8 rows to 4in/10cm measured over patt st using two strands A held tog and one strand B and 15mm (US size 19) needles.

before you start
- There is no need to check your gauge/tension as an exact size is not essential for a scarf. (See page 25 for more about measuring gauge/tension.)
- *For knitting abbreviations, turn to page 127.*

cast on
Using 15mm (US size 19) needles and two strands A held tog, cast on 23 sts.
K one row.
Drop A at side of work and beg zigzag patt as foll:
1st patt row (RS) Using one strand B, k1, sl 2 sts knitwise one at a time onto RH needle, insert tip of LH needle through fronts of 2 slipped sts and k2tog through back of loops—called *slip, slip, knit* or *ssk*—k7, sl 2 sts tog as if to k2tog, k1, lift up 2 slipped sts with tip of LH needle and pass them over st just knit and off RH needle—called *sl2, k1, p2sso*—, k7, k2tog, k1.
2nd patt row Using one strand B, k1, *p1, k3, k next st but don't slip it off LH needle yet, bring yarn to front between 2 needles then to back over RH needle to make an extra st—called *yarn over* or *yo*—, k into same st again and slip it off LH needle, k3*; rep from * to * once more, p1, k1.
Drop B at side of work.
3rd patt row Using two strands A, as first row.
4th patt row Using two strands A, as 2nd row.
Rep 1st–4th patt rows until scarf measures 67in/170cm long or desired length, ending with a 3rd patt row. (Hang scarf to measure it, as this is the length when worn.)

bind/cast off
Using A, bind/cast off all 19 sts loosely knitwise.

finishing touches
Weave in any loose ends or knot them together and clip off the ends close to the knots.
Attach beads to each of the two points at the

bound-/cast-off end of the scarf and the three points at the cast-on end as follows:
Cut a 15¾in/40cm length of B, fold it in half, and pull the loop at the folded end through the tip of the point with the tip of a knitting needle or a crochet hook. Draw the ends of the yarn strand through the loop and pull tight to secure. Thread one small bead and one large bead onto the double strand and knot the end to hold on the beads.

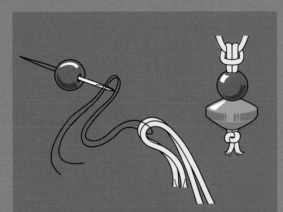

string the beads like this!

Even if your beads have big holes, it may not be that easy to pass knitting yarn through them, especially if you're using two strands of yarn as on the Zigzag Scarf. This method is foolproof. Fold a length of sewing thread in half and pass the two ends through a fine sewing needle. Then just loop the yarn through the loop of sewing thread and draw it through the bead.

alternative beads/colorways

Hunting for exquisite beads is a favorite pastime of mine. It isn't always easy to find just the right color, shape, size, and texture for your finished knitting, so it's sometimes better to start with the beads and choose yarns to complement them.

chenille boas

Worked in a soft cotton chenille, the boa collar pictured right is really fun to knit. The wiggly "arms" are made by casting on and binding/casting off stitches in each row. Any yarn that adds to the cosiness would suit this design—knobbly bouclés or bouclé mixes would look especially good. You can make a long boa scarf from this wiggly pattern as well; just keep on knitting until it's as long as you like (see page 49). If you are a beginner, you could use this pattern to practice casting on and binding/casting off—afterward your fingers will never forget the techniques.

here's how...

Every single row of these boas is worked in the same way, so after you've worked a few you won't have to keep reading the instructions. Two identical layers are knit to form both versions of the boa—the collar (see page 47) and the scarf (see right).

how big is it?
- **Boa collar:** The finished collar measures approximately 34in/86cm long.
- **Boa scarf:** The finished scarf measures approximately 68in/172cm long.

which stitches and techniques?
- Cast on, bind/cast off
- Knit stitch

how much yarn?
Boa collar

MC = chunky chenille yarn in main color
  1 x 3¹/₂oz/100g ball Rowan *Chunky Cotton Chenille* in chosen color

CC = chunky chenille yarn in contrasting color
  small amount Rowan *Chunky Cotton Chenille* in chosen color

Boa scarf

Chunky chenille yarn
  2 x 3¹/₂oz/100g balls Rowan *Chunky Cotton*

try this!

For a more delicate boa collar or scarf, use a single strand of Rowan *Chunky Cotton Chenille* throughout and a pair of 15mm (US size 19) knitting needles.

Chenille in chosen color
(*See page 124 for yarn tips*)

which needles?
Pair of 20mm (US size 35) knitting needles

before you start
- There is no gauge/tension given for this stitch as it is not relevant—an exact size is not essential for the boas. To make them longer or shorter, just work more or fewer rows.
- *For knitting abbreviations, turn to page 127.*

boa collar

cast on
The boa collar pictured on page 47 is made from two identical pieces, stitched together in layers.

First and second pieces (both alike)
*Using 20mm (US size 35) needles and two strands CC held tog, cast on 8 sts using the single cast-on method (see page 17).

1st patt row Bind/cast off 5 sts knitwise, k rem 2 sts; then cast on 5 sts onto RH needle using single cast-on method.

Rep last row to form patt.*
Work 2 rows more in patt.

Next row Bind/cast off 5 sts knitwise, k rem 2 sts; then break off CC, tie ends of CC to two strands MC close to work and cast on 5 sts onto RH needle using single cast-on method.

Cont in patt in MC until there are 15 "arms" along one side from beg and 14 along other side edge—boa measures approximately 30¹/₂in/77cm from beg.

Next row Bind/cast off 5 sts knitwise, k rem 2 sts; then break off MC, tie ends of MC to two strands CC close to work and cast on 5 sts onto RH needle using single cast-on method.

Work 3 rows more in CC.

Using CC, bind/cast off all 8 sts knitwise.

finishing touches

To join, place the two pieces flat and side by side, making sure they are not twisted. Then fold each piece in half lengthwise so that the center stitch is along the fold. Place the folds side by side and sew the pieces together with overcast stitches (see page 120), catching in the center stitches of each piece.

Ties

Cut two strands of CC, each 55in/140cm long, and make a 13in/33cm long twisted cord with them (see page 123), but do not knot the folded end of the cord. Make a second tie in the same way. Attach the ties to the collar where the sections in MC and CC meet—pull the folded end of the cord through the collar with the tip of a knitting needle or a crochet hook, then draw the knotted end through the loop at the folded end and pull tight.

boa scarf

cast on

The boa scarf (right) is made from two identical pieces, stitched together in layers. Work first piece as for collar from * to *, but use two strands of a single color throughout. Work until there are 34 "arms" on one side and 33 on the other, then bind/cast off all 8 sts knitwise. Make second piece in same way.

finishing touches

Place the two pieces together and join as for the boa collar (see Finishing Touches above).

woven-braid scarf

The knitting on this scarf is really easy and the braidmaking is fun. Simple garter stitch is used throughout—you just knit every row in a single color until the scarf is long enough. You can use any color you like for the design, then choose colors for the braids that either contrast sharply, as here, or blend in more subtly. For a quicker finish, dispense with the braids altogether and weave strands of a superthick variegated yarn through the scarf instead, leaving the ends as a fringe.

here's how...

As with most scarves, there's no real need to test your stitch size (gauge/tension) before you start knitting. A scarf a little wider or narrower won't matter and you can just keep knitting the scarf to any length you like.

how big is it?
The finished scarf measures approximately 7½in/19cm wide x 65in/165cm long, excluding the braid fringe.

which stitches?
Garter stitch

how much yarn?
MC = fine mohair yarn in main color
2 x 1oz/25g balls Rowan *Kid Silk Haze* (black—shade no. 599—or chosen color)
A, **B**, and **C** = small amounts of three contrasting colors for braids/plaits (or three contrasting groups of shades) in yarns of your choice
(*See page 124 for yarn tips*)

try this!

- When knitting with mohair on fat needles keep the knitting fairly loose—you'll find that your loops will slide more easily along the needles if you do.

- The Woven-braid Scarf is worked with four strands of a very fine mohair. However, if you decide to use a medium-weight mohair you'll only need two strands.

which needles?
Pair of 12mm (US size 17) knitting needles

any extras?
Sewing thread to match MC, for securing braids

what gauge/tension?
9 sts to 4in/10cm measured over garter st using four strands MC held tog and 12mm (US size 17) needles.

before you start
- You can make each braid/plait from a single color or use groups of toning colors. The three braid colors here were based around three shades of Rowan *Summer Tweed*—raspberry (shade no. 528), apricot (shade no. 509), and mauve (shade no. 510). Some strands of scrap yarns in toning colors were added in with these.
- *For knitting abbreviations, turn to page 127.*

cast on
Using 12mm (US size 17) needles and four strands MC held tog, cast on 17 sts. (Take one strand of yarn from the inside and outside of each ball.)
Work in garter st (k every row) until scarf measures approximately 65in/165cm from cast-on edge. (The scarf is stretchy, so hang it to measure true length.)

bind/cast off
Bind/cast off all 17 sts loosely knitwise.

finishing touches
Weave in any loose ends on the scarf.
Make four braids in chosen colors, each ¼–³⁄₈in/6–8mm wide and 77in/196cm long. If using Rowan *Summer Tweed*, use two to three strands of yarn for

each of the three sections of the braid. Cut strands of yarn for the braids 3½yd/3.2m long.
Position the braids on the scarf 3 sts apart—through the 3rd, 7th, 11th, and 15th stitches across the width. Start at the cast-on edge and weave the braids in and out every 4th row along the length of the scarf. Knot the ends of the braids at the cast-on edge of the scarf and adjust so that they form a 5in/13cm fringe. Catch each braid in place with sewing thread, making a few invisible stitches into the cast-on edge.
Then trim and knot the fringe along the other end to the same length; secure as before.

choosing braid/plait yarns

Mixing yarns to produce original shades is best done by trial and error, so test your attempts with short strands before making the long braids for the scarf. I used leftover yarns to create the colored braids for this scarf. The beautiful shades of Rowan *Summer Tweed* were the starting point for creating just the right colors (see Before You Start on previous page). Wool tapestry yarn or other embroidery threads are also a good source of color for your braids. They come in a vast range of hues.

pompom scarf

Made in a jiffy, this wool scarf is worked in just nine rows on superfat needles. It's short, too, which makes it even quicker than you'd imagine. Use all the spare time you have left over to concentrate on making perfect, pert little pompoms to hang from the ends—simple instructions for making pompoms are given on page 57. Alternatively, look for some enticing chunky, lightweight beads to replace the pompoms. The texture of the scarf is simple single ribbing (knit one, purl one alternately), which forms ridges across the scarf.

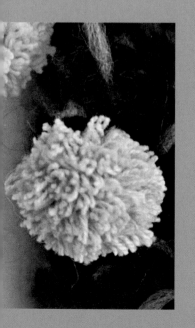

here's how...

The horizontal texture on this scarf comes from the fact that the single ribbing (knit one, purl one) is worked from end to end rather than side to side in the normal way. For a masculine version, make the scarf longer and omit the pompoms.

how big is it?

The finished scarf measures approximately 5in/13cm wide x 34½in/88cm long, excluding the pompom fringe.

which stitches?

Single ribbing (k1, p1)

how much yarn?

MC = superchunky bicolor wool yarn in main color
  1 x 3½oz/100g ball Rowan *Big Wool*
  (black and gray—shade no. 11—or chosen color)
A and **B** = medium-weight cotton yarn in two contrasting colors for pompoms
  small amounts of Rowan *All Seasons Cotton*
  in two colors (lime—shade no. 197—and
  turquoise—shade no. 185—or chosen colors)
(*See page 124 for yarn tips*)

which needles?

Pair of 20mm (US size 35) knitting needles

what gauge/tension?

5 sts to 4in/10cm measured over single ribbing using MC and 20mm (US size 35) needles.

before you start

- There is no need to check your gauge/tension before beginning as an exact size is not essential for a scarf. But you can use the gauge/tension to

alternative colorway

Personalize your scarf by choosing your own colors. A bicolor yarn makes interesting spotted pompoms. If you add in a second color when making a pompom, you can create a stripe.

calculate how many more stitches to add for a longer scarf.
- *For knitting abbreviations, turn to page 127.*

cast on
Using 20mm (US size 35) needles and MC, cast on 44 sts loosely using the double cast-on method.
1st rib row *K1, p1; rep from *.
Rep last row 8 times more.

bind/cast off
Bind/cast off all 44 sts loosely while working sts in rib patt.

finishing touches
Weave in any loose ends.
Make a total of 10 pompoms, using A and B (see right for how to make pompoms). Trim pompoms to 1¼in/3cm in diameter (leave a long end on the strong yarn at the center of each pompom to use to tie the pompom to the hanging strand of MC).
Tie each pompom to a 24in/60cm length of MC, positioning the knot as close to the center of the pompom as possible to hide it. Trim the ends close to the knot.
Stitch the hanging pompoms to the ends of the scarf alternating the colors and varying the lengths of the hanging strands.

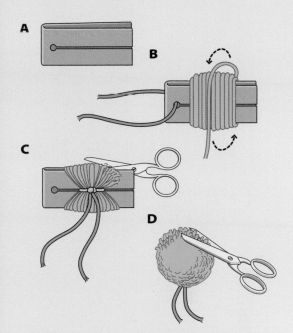

make quick pompoms!

You may have an excellent pompom-making tool—and there are several types to choose from—but if, like me, you find the one you have slows the process down, try this technique. Cut a 5–6in/13–15cm long strip of cardboard as wide as the desired diameter of your pompom (1¼in/3cm for the Pompom Scarf). Fold the cardboard in half widthwise and poke a hole through the center of both layers near the fold. Then cut through the center of the strip to the holes as shown (A). Cut a length of strong yarn for tying the pompom and thread it through the holes. Next, wrap the yarn round and round the cardboard until there's enough yarn for a nice plump pompom (B). Slide the other end of the tying strand through the cut slots and knot tightly around the pompom. Cut through the pompom yarn at the top and bottom, passing the scissor blades between the layers (C). Slide the pompom off the cardboard and trim the shape to neatly round it (D).

If you want to try out "rag" knitting, this is the project for you. The jewel-colored "yarns" are made from narrow strips of silk fabric, and the rough edges of the silk create an excitingly vibrant texture. Made up of two simple garter stitch rectangles, the bag can be knitted up in no time at all. The rectangles are stitched together

rag shoulder bag

with an ordinary sewing needle and thread, and, to create the stand-up shape, the two bottom corners are pinched and stitched together before the bag is turned right side out. A braided strap makes a great finishing touch, but you could use a readymade cord for it if you prefer.

here's how...

This bag is worked with seven colors of silk. Use even more colors if you like. Luckily, there are no stray ends to weave in (as with other multicolored knitting), because the ends are all knotted at the edges and hidden inside.

how big is it?

The finished bag measures 8¹/₄in/21cm tall x 8¹/₂in/21cm wide x 2¹/₂in/6cm deep. The shoulder strap measures 26³/₄in/68cm long (adjustable).

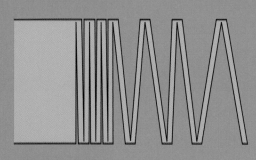

make your own yarn!

If your fabric tears easily, the quickest way to prepare your knitting strips is to tear them. They look just as good as cut strips when knitted up. To make a continuous strip of "rag" yarn, first straighten the end of your length of fabric. Then start at the selvage and tear or cut a strip of the required width, stopping near the selvage. It is generally best to stop at a distance from the edge of the fabric that is half the width of the strip. Turn and tear or cut in the opposite direction, stopping near the edge as before. Tear or cut back and forth in this way. (For a quick cutting method, see page 95.)

which stitches?
Garter stitch

how much "yarn"?
Douppioni silk for rag "yarn" as foll:
A = orange-red
    51in/130cm of 44in/112cm wide fabric
B = fuchsia
    51in/130cm of 44in/112cm wide fabric
C = dull blue
    6in/15cm of 44in/112cm wide fabric
D = red
    24in/60cm of 44in/112cm wide fabric
E = tangerine
    12in/30cm of 44in/112cm wide fabric
F = lavender blue
    6in/15cm of 44in/112cm wide fabric
G = turquoise
    6in/15cm of 44in/112cm wide fabric

which needles?
Pair of 15mm (US size 19) knitting needles

any extras?
- Sewing thread for joining knitted pieces
- 11³/₄in/30cm by 22in/55cm piece of douppioni silk in chosen color for lining and matching thread

what gauge/tension?
5¹/₂ sts and 9¹/₂ rows to 4in/10cm measured over garter st using a 1¹/₂–1³/₄in/4–4.5cm wide strip of silk and 15mm (US size 19) needles.

before you start
- Cut (or tear) your fabric rag strips 1¹/₂–1³/₄in/ 4–4.5cm wide (see left and page 95 for how to prepare strips). Cut a small ball of rag strips to use

knitting with fabric strips

Douppioni silk is great for "rag" knitting. It has a
lovely texture and comes in jewel colors. It comes
either in plain colors or ones "shot" with another
color. The "shot" colors run lengthwise on the fabric
and make it change color when the light hits it at
different angles. As you can see on the strips above
the lavender blue used for the bag is shot with
fuchsia, the tangerine is shot with red, the fuchsia is
shot with black, and the turquoise is shot with green.

for testing your gauge/tension and then adjust the width of the strips if necessary.

- Cast on 9 stitches and work a square of garter stitch using 15mm (US size 19) needles and a fabric strip to check your stitch size. (See page 25 for more about gauge/tension.)
- Draw a rectangle 9 1/2in/24cm tall by 10 3/4in/ 27cm wide on a large piece of paper. This is a template for the size of the two knitted pieces needed for the bag. The knitting is quite "giving," so the template is useful for testing the width and length as you knit.
- *For knitting abbreviations, turn to page 127.*

cast on

The bag is made in two pieces—a front and a back.
Front and back (both alike)
Using 15mm (US size 19) needles and A (orange-red), cast on 15 sts.

try this!

- **For a less frayed effect, knit this bag using cotton strips in the colors of your choice. Cut the strips 1 1/2in/4cm wide. If you're on a tight budget, use fabric scraps.**

- **Use a strong thread, like buttonhole thread, to stitch the knitted pieces together.**

- **Stitch a flat knitted strap to the bag as an alternative. Using 12mm (US size 17) needles and rag strips of A, cast on three stitches. Work in garter stitch (knit every row) to the desired length and bind/cast off. Stretch the knitted strap when measuring, to test what its true length will be when in use.**

1st stripe row (WS) Using A, knit.
2nd stripe row (RS) Using A, knit.
Before turning knitting to start next row, mark this side of the knitting (the RS) with a safety pin.
Now work 23 rows more in stripes, cutting off each color before changing to the next and knotting the strip ends tog at the edge of the knitting (see page 71), and cont in garter st (k every row) as foll:
Work 3 rows more in A, then work 2 rows B, 1 row C, 1 row D, 1 row E, 2 rows B, 1 row E, 2 rows A, 1 row D, 1 row B, 1 row F, 3 rows B, 1 row G, 1 row D, 2 rows A, so ending with a WS row. 25 rows have been worked from cast-on edge and piece should measure 10 3/4in/27cm.

bind/cast off

Using B and with RS facing, bind/cast off all 15 sts knitwise and fairly tightly.
Do not trim the frayed thread until the bag is stitched tog.

finishing touches

Using a sewing needle and thread and with right sides facing, sew the front and back pieces together around three sides, matching the stripes and leaving the edges with the bound-/cast-off stitches (top end) open. Before turning right side out, mark a point 1 1/4in/3cm from the bottom and side seams in each of the two lower corners of the bag, and on the back and the front. Pinch the bottom seam and side seam together at the two corners to form a triangular point (see shape on page 121) and stitch from marked point to marked point as shown. Turn the bag right side out.
Lining
Take the 11 3/4in/30cm by 22in/55cm piece of lining fabric and zigzag stitch the raw edges on the sewing machine to prevent fraying. Then fold the fabric in half widthwise and stitch 1/2in/1.5cm side seams. Mark and stitch across the triangular points at each lower corner of the lining as for the bag (see page

121). Fold 1½in/3.5cm to the wrong side around the top edge and pin. Insert the lining in the bag and stitch to the bag around the top edge.

Strap

For the braided/plaited shoulder strap, prepare two 1¾in/4.5cm wide strips each in fabrics A, B, and D. Use 59in/1.5m long strips for a 26¾in/68cm strap (or 78in/2m strips for a 41in/104cm strap). Knot together one length each of A, B, and D, 2in/5cm from one end. Then braid/plait the strips together for 4½in/11cm. Knot together and braid/plait the three remaining strips in the same way. Then join the strips together into a single braid/plait, working with the two A strips together, the two B strips together and the two D strips together. Work this thicker strap for 18in/46cm (or 32¼in/82cm for the longer strap). Next, separate the strands into two separate sections again and work for another 4½in/11cm. Knot the ends of the strap and trim the ends to 2in/5cm from the knot. Sew the finished strap to the outside of the bag, positioning each knotted end at the top edge of the bag, ¾in/2cm from a side seam.

Tidy the knitting by trimming off any frayed fabric threads that are hanging off the bag.

making the bag strap
The braided/plaited bag shoulder strap is made with fabric strips. It starts with two thin braids, then these are combined to make the thicker main section of the strap, and divided again to end with two thin braids.

star-stitch bag

The striking star-stitch pattern on this drawstring shoulder bag is much easier to knit than it looks—only one color of yarn is used in each row. Made from two simple square pieces of knitting, the pattern is within the reach of a beginner. You can work the bag in the bold contrasts of a black chunky cotton chenille and a white chunky wool, as shown, or choose a more subdued color scheme, if you prefer. For an attractive accent, find some enticing beads to string onto the drawstring tassels.

here's how...

You could also use the star-stitch pattern on this shoulder bag for a cushion cover. See the instructions in Before You Start for how many stitches to cast on to make bigger pieces of knitting.

how big is it?
The finished bag measures 8¼in/21cm deep from drawstring eyelets to bottom edge, excluding top ruffle. It is 8¼in/21cm wide.

which stitches?
- Stockinette/stocking stitch (St st)
- Simple bicolor pattern stitch

how much yarn?
MC = chunky chenille yarn in main color
   1 x 3½oz/100g ball Rowan *Chunky Cotton Chenille*
   (black—shade no. 367—or chosen color)
CC = chunky wool yarn in contrasting color
   1 x 3½oz/100g ball Rowan *Polar*
   (off-white—shade no. 645—or chosen color)
(*See page 124 for yarn tips*)

which needles?
Pair each of 12mm and 15mm (US sizes 17 and 19) knitting needles

any extras?
- 64–72 small glass beads (5mm in diameter) for tassels, with holes big enough to fit single strand of chenille yarn
- Black fabric and sewing thread for lining

what gauge/tension?
9½ sts to 4in/10cm measured over patt st using two strands MC held tog and one strand CC and 15mm (US size 19) needles.

before you start
- It is not important to exactly match recommended gauge/tension. But it is a good idea to practice the pattern stitch before beginning. Cast on a multiple of 3 sts plus 2 sts extra and purl one row. Then work 1st–4th patt rows below.
- *For knitting abbreviations, turn to page 127.*

cast on
The bag is made in two pieces—a back and a front.
Front and back (both alike)
Using 12mm (US size 17) needles and two strands MC, cast on 20 sts using the double cast-on method. Beg with a k row, work 6 rows in St st, so ending wth a p (WS) row.
Change to 15mm (US size 19) needles and beg patt as foll:
1st patt row (RS) Using two strands MC, k1, *k3, insert tip of LH needle into first of 3 sts just knit and lift it up and pass it over 2nd and 3rd sts and off RH needle*; rep from * to *, ending with k1. (Drop MC at side of work.)
2nd patt row Using one strand CC, p1, *insert tip of RH needle from behind under "running strand" (formed with two strands MC) between st just worked and next st and p this strand, p2*; rep from * to *, ending with p1.
3rd patt row Using one strand CC, k2, *k3, insert tip of LH needle into first of 3 sts just knit and lift it up and pass it over 2nd and 3rd sts and off RH needle*; rep from * to *. (Drop CC at side of work.)
4th patt row Using two strands MC, p2, *insert tip of RH needle from behind under running strand between st just worked and next st and p this strand, p2*; rep from * to *.
Rep 1st–4th patt rows twice more, so ending with a WS row. Break off CC.

Change to 12mm (US size 17) needles.
Using two strands MC and beg with a k row, work
6 rows in St st, so ending with a WS row.
Cont with MC, make eyelet holes for drawstring
as foll:
Eyelet row (RS) K3, bring yarn to front between
two needles then to back over RH needle to make
an extra st—called *yarn over* or *yo*—, k2tog, [yo,
k2tog] 7 times, k1. (20 sts)
Work 7 rows in garter st (k every row), so ending
with a WS row.

bind/cast off
Using one strand CC, bind/cast off all 20 sts knitwise.

finishing touches
Draw a paper pattern for the lining, the same size
as the front (from the cast-on edge to the eyelet
holes). Then add a seam allowance of 1/2in/1.5cm
around the two sides and the bottom, and a hem
allowance of 1 1/2in/4cm at the top. Using this
pattern, cut two pieces of lining fabric. Stitch the
pieces together around three sides. Fold the hem
to the wrong side and press (see page 121).
With the right sides of the knitted front and back
together, sew the side seams, leaving the top and
bottom edges open. Turn right side out and sew
the bottom seam on the outside using double-sided
backstitch (see page 120).
Insert the lining and stitch in place just below the
eyelet holes.
Drawstrings
For the first drawstring, cut three 3 1/4yd/3m strands
of MC and use these to make a twisted cord (see
page 123). Knot each end of the cord so that the
cord measures 27 1/2in/70cm long between the two
knots and there are equal long ends beyond the

making beaded tassels
For the bead tassels, unravel the six strands
of MC beyond each knot on the drawstrings,
thread two or three beads onto each strand,
and knot the ends to secure the beads.

knots at each end (the extra at each end is for
knotting on the beads).
Make a second drawstring in the same way and
thread the drawstrings through the eyelets so that
the ends of one drawstring are at one side seam and
the ends of the second drawstring at the other side
seam. Make the beaded tassels (see above).
Strap
Make a twisted cord for the strap in the same way,
but use five strands of MC. Trim the cord to the
desired length and stitch to the inside of the bag at
the side seams, poking it through the gap left in the
lining hem. Stitch the lining closed.

This rag-knitting shopping bag is made up from three simple rectangular pieces worked in garter stitch—a back, a front, and a base. It has no complicated shaping at all. The "yarn" is created

rag shopping bag

from narrow strips of fabric, so you can get as much enjoyment from collecting your fabrics as from knitting the bag. Cotton patchwork fabrics, preferably in sales, are a good source. When I knit another one, though, I shall make the yarn strips from old shirts in soft colors, collected from friends or bought at charity shops. Then it will be a truly planet-friendly "rag" creation.

here's how...

Knitting this bag is a perfect way to use up fabric remnants. If you decide to use scraps, simply ignore the instructions for the stripe pattern. Instead cut your scraps into random-length strips and knot them together. Push the knots to the wrong side as they are worked into the knitting.

how big is it?
The finished bag measures approximately 12¼in/31cm tall and the base of the bag approximately 6in/15cm x 12½in/32cm.

which stitches?
Garter stitch

how much "yarn"?
Fabric for rag "yarn" as foll:

MC = medium gold
   6¾yd/6.2m of 53in/135cm wide cotton, *or*
   8¼yd/7.5m of 44in/112cm wide cotton

A = dull blue
   ½yd/40cm of 53in/135cm wide cotton, *or*
   ¾yd/50cm of 44in/112cm wide cotton

B = dark gold
   3½yd/3.2m of 44in/112cm wide cotton or silk

C = maroon and gold plaid
   1½yd/1.2m of 60in/153cm wide cotton, *or*
   2yd/1.7m of 44in/112cm wide cotton

which needles?
Pair of 15mm (US size 19) knitting needles

any extras?
- Strong sewing thread, for joining knitted pieces together
- 5yd/4.5m grosgrain ribbon 1¼in/3cm wide for handle (optional)

what gauge/tension?
5½ sts and 10 rows to 4in/10cm measured over garter st stripe patt using 15mm (US size 19) needles.

before you start
- For the bag pictured, cotton curtain lining was used for MC and A, silk douppioni for B, and a plaid shirt fabric for C. But you can use any fabrics that will give a firm knitted texture. Absolute beginners should use patchwork-cotton or shirt-cotton weight fabrics, as cotton curtain lining can be a bit stiff to handle.
- Cut (or tear) strips 3in/7.5cm wide for a cotton-curtain-lining or shirt-fabric weights. For finer cottons or silk, cut the strips 3¾in/9.5cm wide (see pages 60 and 95 for tips on cutting). Make a small ball of fabric strips to use for testing your gauge/tension and then adjust the width of the strips if necessary.
- Cast on 9 stitches and work a square of garter stitch using 15mm (US size 19) needles and a fabric strip to check your stitch size. (See page 25 for more about gauge/tension.)
- The first row of each piece is a bit stiff to work, but the knitting becomes easier in the following rows.
- *For knitting abbreviations, turn to page 127.*

cast on
The bag is made in three pieces—a front, a back, and a base piece.

Front and back (both alike)
Using 15mm (US size 19) needles and A, cast on 28 sts loosely, using the single cast-on method (see page 17).

Using MC, work 4 rows in garter st (k every row).

Cont in garter st throughout, work in stripes as foll:

2 rows B.

2 rows C.

2 rows B.

4 rows MC.

2 rows B.

2 rows C.

2 rows B.

9 rows MC, so ending with a RS row. (Piece measures approximately 12¹/₄in/31cm tall.)

Using MC, bind/cast off knitwise.

Base piece

Using 15mm (US size 19) needles and MC, cast on 8 sts loosely.

Work 30 rows in garter st. (Test that the bound-/cast-off edges of the front and back pieces will fit around the outside edge of the base piece and adjust length of base if necessary.)

Bind/cast off knitwise.

finishing touches

Using a sewing needle and thread, sew the front and back together along the side seams. Work edge-to-edge seams from the right side, carefully hiding the slip stitches and matching the stripes. Then pin the bound-/cast-off edge of the bag to the base piece and stitch in place.

Handle

For the handle, make a 1¹/₄in/3cm wide band from the remaining fabric (MC) or use grosgrain ribbon. For a grosgrain handle, cut two 88¹/₂in/225cm lengths of grosgrain, lay the lengths on top of each other, and stitch together along each side. For a fabric handle, cut a 88¹/₂in/225cm long strip of fabric 5in/12cm wide, piecing strips together to make up the length. Fold the band in half lengthwise with wrong sides together. Then open

A

B

knot on a new rag strip like this!

Join on a new strip in "rag" knitting by knotting it on before you start a row. Tie the knot really close to the knitting and pull it tight (A). Trim off the ends near the knot (B). You can join on a new strip in the middle of a row like this, too—just make sure the knot is pushed to the wrong side of the work if you don't want it to show on the front.

out, fold each raw edge to the center, and press. Fold in half lengthwise again and topstitch along each side of the band.

Weave the handle in and out of the bag as shown, making sure that the strap is on the outside of the knitting over the base of the bag. Join the ends of the strap under the base of the bag.

Tidy the knitting by trimming off any frayed fabric threads that are hanging off the bag.

tweed
handbag

Here's something to try once you've made a few supereasy knits. Worked in a wool tweed with a flap border of cotton yarns, this garter stitch bag is lined in a contrasting color fabric. Making it is a good way to learn the basics of simple shaping and will improve your ability to follow a knitting pattern. If you want something easier to knit, turn it into a much simpler bag by omitting the gusset and shaping (as explained on the next page). You could add a long shoulder strap as well.

here's how...

To make this into a bag for beginners, omit the gusset and shaping. Cast on 21 stitches and knit two rectangles for the back and front—the back longer to include the flap. Make a twisted cord for the strap.

how big is it?
The finished bag measures 8³/₄in/22cm wide at base x 7in/17.5cm tall.

which stitches?
Garter stitch

how much yarn?
MC = chunky wool yarn in main color
  2 x 3¹/₂oz/100g balls Rowan *Yorkshire Tweed* (olive—shade no. 557—or chosen color)
A = lightweight silk and cotton blend yarn in first contrasting color
  small amount Rowan *Summer Tweed* (lilac—shade no. 501—or chosen color)
B = lightweight silk and cotton blend yarn in second contrasting color
  small amount Rowan *Summer Tweed* (mauve—shade no. 510—or chosen color)
C = chunky wool yarn in third contrasting color
  small amount Rowan *Polar* (dusty green—shade no. 645—or chosen color)

which needles?
Pair of 12mm (US size 17) knitting needles

any extras?
Fabric and matching sewing thread, for lining

what gauge/tension?
9¹/₂ sts and 14¹/₂ rows to 4in/10cm over garter st using two strands MC and 12mm (US size 17) needles.

before you start
- To check your stitch size, work a square of garter stitch using 12mm (US size 17) needles and two strands MC (see page 25).
- *For knitting abbreviations, turn to page 127.*

cast on
The bag is made in three pieces—a front, a back (with flap extension), and a piece for gusset/handle.
Back
Using 12mm (US size 17) needles and two strands MC, cast on 21 sts using the double cast-on method. K one row.
1st row (RS) P1, k19, p1. (Use a contrasting yarn to mark this row as RS of work before turning.)
2nd row (WS) Sl 1 knitwise, k19, sl 1 knitwise.
3rd–7th rows Rep 1st–2nd rows twice, then rep 1st row once more.
8th row (dec row) Sl 1 knitwise, k2tog, k15, k2tog, sl 1 knitwise. (19 sts)
9th row P1, k17, p1.
10th row Sl 1 knitwise, k17, sl 1 knitwise.
11th–15th rows Rep 9th–10th rows twice, then rep 9th row once more.
16th row (dec row) Sl 1 knitwise, k2tog, k13, k2tog, sl 1 knitwise. (17 sts)
17th row P1, k15, p1.
18th row Sl 1 knitwise, k15, sl 1 knitwise.
19th–22nd rows Rep 17th–18th rows twice.**
Mark each end of last row (for last row of back).
Cont on back to form flap extension as foll:
23rd–32nd rows Rep 17th–18th rows 5 times.
Break off MC.
33rd row Using two strands A and one strand B held tog, as 17th row.
34th row Using two strands A and one strand B held tog, as 18th row.

here's how...

The Colorwork Knapsack is knitted following a chart (see page 77). In intarsia knitting a separate ball of yarn is used for each area of color to avoid loose, "floating" strands across the back of the knitting. If you're not ready for colorwork knitting, make the Plain Knapsack instead (see pages 80–81).

how big is it?
The finished knapsacks measure 12¼in/31cm wide x 13½in/34cm tall.

which stitches?
- Stockinette/stocking stitch (St st)
- Garter stitch

how much yarn?
Plain and colorwork knapsacks
MC = variegated wool and nylon tape yarn in main color
   3 x 3½oz/100g hanks Colinette *Tagliatelli*
   (shade no. 147 or chosen color)
A = medium-weight cotton yarn to strengthen drawstrings
   small amount of Rowan *All Seasons Cotton*
   (shade no. 165—or shade to match chosen MC)

try this!
- When making really long twisted cords like the ones for this knapsack, get a friend to help you fold it in half when twisting together.

- If you're in a hurry, use a readymade drawstring cord instead of making your own.

Colorwork knapsack only
CC = lightweight silk and cotton blend yarn in contrasting color
   1 x 1¾oz/50g hank Rowan *Summer Tweed*
   (lilac—shade no. 501—or chosen color)
(*See page 124 for yarn tips*)

which needles?
Pair of 12mm (US size 17) knitting needles

any extras?
Plain and colorwork knapsacks
- Small amount of fabric and matching sewing thread for lining
- Two metal curtain rings ¾in/2cm in diameter
Plain knapsack only
- Small amount of felt in contrasting color and iron-on bonding web

what gauge/tension?
9½ sts to 4in/10cm measured over St st using two strands MC and 12mm (US size 17) needles.

before you start
- It is not important to exactly match recommended gauge/tension if you are happy to have a bag of a slightly different size.
- The *Tagliatelli* yarn is very stretchy, so be sure to wind your balls loosely from the hanks to avoid damaging the yarn.
- When working from the colorwork chart, read RS (knit) rows from right to left and WS (purl) rows from left to right. Use a separate length of yarn for each block of color and twist yarns around each other when changing colors to avoid creating holes (see page 79).
- *For knitting abbreviations, turn to page 127.*

colorwork knapsack

cast on

The Colorwork Knapsack on page 77 is made in two pieces—a back and a front.

Front and back (both alike)

Using 12mm (US size 17) needles and two strands MC, cast on 30 sts using the double cast-on method (see page 18).

Work 3 rows in garter st (k every row).**

Beg with a k row, work 2 rows St st.

Then beg working from chart on next row as foll:

3rd chart row (RS) K19 MC, k6 CC, k5 MC.

4th chart row (WS) P5 MC, p6 CC, p19 MC.

Cont in this way in St st foll chart until 39th chart row has been completed, so ending with a RS row.

Using MC, work 5 rows in garter st (k every row).

bind/cast off

Bind/cast off all 30 sts knitwise.

finishing touches

Draw a paper pattern for the lining, the same size as the front. Then add a seam allowance of $^1/_2$in/1.5cm around the two sides and bottom, and a hem allowance of 2in/5cm at the top for the drawstring channel. Use this pattern to cut two pieces of lining fabric. With the right sides of the knitted front and back together, join the seam beginning and ending below the garter stitch border at the top. Turn right side out. Stitch the lining pieces together around three sides, beginning and ending the seam $3^1/_2$in/9cm from top to allow for the drawstring channel. Press the seam allowances at top of side seams to the wrong side. For the drawstring channel, press $^1/_4$in/1cm then $1^3/_4$in/4cm to the wrong side. Stitch the drawstring channel in place

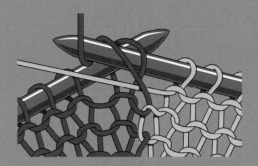

change yarns like this!

Intarsia knitting is much easier than it looks. Each area of color uses a separate length or ball of yarn. Where the colors meet the yarns are twisted or looped around each other. When changing colors on both wrong side and right side rows, wrap the next color around the last color as shown above.

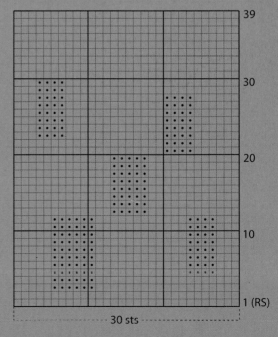

□ = MC   ⊡ = CC

close to the first fold, leaving the ends open. Insert the lining in the knapsack and stitch in place.

Drawstrings

For the first drawstring, cut 5½yd/5m strands—four lengths of MC and three lengths of A. Make a 63in/160cm long twisted cord (see page 123), knotting the cut end and leaving the folded end unknotted (so it can be threaded into the channel). Make a second drawstring in the same way and thread the drawstrings through the channel so that the ends of one drawstring are at one side seam and the ends of the second drawstring are at the other side seam. (You can use a big crochet hook to draw them through, hooking it into the folded end of the cord.)

Stitch one metal ring to each bottom corner of the bag, pass the ends of one drawstring through each ring and knot them to keep them from slipping out (knot them to each other or to the ring).

plain knapsack

cast on

The Plain Knapsack on the right is made in two pieces—a back and a front.

Front and back (both alike)

Cast on and work as for Colorwork Knapsack to **. Then beg with a k row, work 39 rows St st, so ending with a RS row.

Work 5 rows in garter st (k every row).

bind/cast off

Bind/cast off all 30 sts knitwise.

finishing touches

Follow the Finishing Touches for the Colorwork Knapsack. Then make decorative felt circles as explained left, arrange them along the bottom of the bag, and knot them on with a single strand of MC. Trim off the yarn ends close to the knots.

making circles for plain knapsack

To make the circle decorations for the Plain Knapsack, first fuse two layers of felt together with bonding web. Then cut eight circles 1½in/4cm in diameter from the felt. Cut two ¼in/1cm slits, ½in/1.5cm apart at the center of each circle. Attach as explained right.

string bags

With giant-needle knitting you can make lacy textures just by working your knits and purls with a medium-weight yarn on really fat needles—the Garter Stitch Bag on the right is made in this way. The Lace String Bag (see page 86) and the Lace-rib Bag (see page 87) are worked in simple lace pattern stitches on slightly thinner needles. Each of the three bags is made from two simple rectangles and there are three different handle types, too. I am fascinated by cotton string bags and think they are both stylish and amazingly practical. You can scrunch them up in your handbag and pull them out on the way home from work to carry your shopping in.

here's how...

When knitting these bags I realized that the soft cotton lacy textures would make great scarves as well. To turn a bag texture into a scarf, cast on the number of stitches recommended for one side of the bag and knit until it's the desired length.

how big is it?
- **Garter stitch bag:** The finished bag measures 12in/30cm wide x 9in/23cm long.
- **Lace string bag:** The finished bag measures 12in/30cm wide x 10in/25.5cm long.
- **Lace-rib bag:** The finished bag measures 12in/30cm wide x 10in/25.5cm long.

(*The bags are stretchy and not easy to measure exactly.*)

which stitches?
- Garter stitch pattern on garter stitch bag
- Lace stitches on "lace" bags

how much yarn?
Garter stitch bag

MC = medium-weight cotton yarn in main color
> 1 x 1³/₄oz/50g ball Rowan *All Seasons Cotton* in chosen color

CC = medium-weight cotton yarn in contrasting color
> 1 x 1³/₄oz/50g ball Rowan *All Seasons Cotton* in chosen color

Lace string bag or Lace-rib bag

MC = medium-weight cotton yarn in main color
> 2 x 1³/₄oz/50g balls Rowan *All Seasons Cotton* in chosen color

CC = medium-weight cotton yarn in contrasting color
> 1 x 1³/₄oz/50g ball Rowan *All Seasons Cotton* in chosen color

(*See page 124 for yarn tips*)

which needles?
Garter stitch bag: Pair of 10mm and 12mm (US sizes 15 and 17) knitting needles
Lace string bag: Pair of 10mm (US size 15) knitting needles
Lace-rib bag: Pair of 10mm (US size 15) knitting needles and two 9mm (US size 13) double-pointed needles

any extras?
For Lace String Bag only, pair of circular wooden ring handles, 5in/13cm in diameter and painted with acrylics in desired color

what gauge/tension?
Garter stitch bag: Approximately 8¹/₂ sts to 4in/10cm measured over garter st patt using 12mm (US size 17) needles.
Lace string bag: Approximately 10 sts to 4in/10cm measured over patt using 10mm (US size 15) needles.
Lace-rib bag: Approximately 11 sts to 4in/10cm measured over patt using 10mm (US size 15) knitting needles.

try this!
To avoid having to count rows twice—once when working the back and once when working the front—work both the front and the back at the same time. If you only have one ball of yarn, take one strand from the outside of the ball for the front and the other strand from the inside of the ball for the back.

before you start

- There is no need to check your gauge/tension before beginning as an exact size for the bags is not essential.
- You can make your bag bigger if you like, but remember it stretches—so test it as you knit.
- Round wooden handbag handles are available in craft shops, or use two wooden embroidery rings 5in/13cm in diameter.
- *For knitting abbreviations, turn to page 127.*

garter stitch bag

cast on

The Garter Stitch Bag pictured on page 83 is made in two pieces—a back and a front.

Front and back (both alike)

Using 12mm (US size 17) needles and MC, cast on 25 sts loosely using the double cast-on method (see page 18).

K one row.

Beg garter st patt as foll:

1st, 2nd, and 3rd patt rows Knit.

4th patt row *K1 wrapping yarn twice around RH needle; rep from * to end.

5th patt row Knit in usual way (without wrapping twice around needle), dropping second wrap from last row on each st.

Rep 1st–5th rows 3 times more.

K one row.

Dec on next row as foll:

Next row (dec row) *K2tog, k3tog; rep from *. (10 sts)

Cut off MC.

Tie handle

Using 10mm (US size 15) needles and two strands CC, work handle as foll:

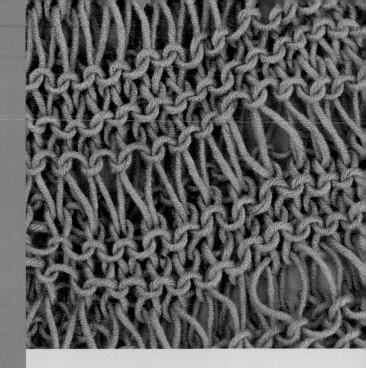

garter stitch bag

Knitting a thin yarn on fat needles creates a lovely open texture. To make the Garter Stitch Bag even lacier, I have added huge loops by wrapping the yarn twice around the needle and dropping the extra wrap in the next row.

Next row (RS) Before working bag sts, cast on 14 sts onto RH needle, using the single cast-on method (see page 17); k10 sts of bag, cast on 14 sts. (38 sts)

K one row.

P one row.

bind/cast off

Bind/cast off all 38 sts loosely knitwise.

finishing touches

With the right sides facing, sew the back and front together, beginning and ending the seam 4–4¼in/10–10.5cm from the handles. (To keep the seam stretchy, work two overcast stitches at each protruding "pip" on the edge of the knitting to secure the yarn, and leave the yarn slack between pips.) Turn right side out. Knot each handle.

lace string bag

cast on

The Lace String Bag on the left is made in two pieces—a back and a front.

Front and back (both alike)

Using 10mm (US size 15) needles and MC, cast on 30 sts. (The patt is worked over an even number of sts.)

1st patt row K1, *bring yarn to front between 2 needles then to back over RH needle to make an extra st—called *yarn over* or *yo*—, k2tog; rep from *, ending with k1.

Rep last row to form patt.

Work 17 rows more in patt.

Drop MC at side of work.

Change to CC and work 2 rows in patt.

Cut off CC.

Change to MC and work 12 rows in patt.

Hem for handle

K 3 rows. (Mark each end of last row with a strand of contrasting yarn.)

P one row.

K one row (RS).

P one row (WS).

bind/cast off

Bind/cast off all 30 sts knitwise, leaving a long loose end for stitching bag top to wooden handle.

finishing touches

Place the hem of the front around a handle, with the stockinette/stocking stitch side facing outward. Stitch the bound-/cast-off edge to the heads of the stitches at the top of the marked row. Sew a handle to the back in the same way. With the right sides of the front and back together, stitch the side seams from the bottom edge to within 4³/4in–5in/12–13cm of the handle, leaving the bottom edge open.

Lace a length of yarn through the bottom edge, catching in a single strand from every other cast-on stitch, draw up tight, and secure. Turn right side out.

lace string bag

The Lace String Bag above is worked in a really simple lace pattern. It creates a stretchy fabric perfect for a string bag. The softness of the yarn and stitch also make it ideal for a scarf.

lace-rib bag

cast on

The Lace-rib Bag on the right is made in two pieces—a back and a front.

Front and back (both alike)

Using 10mm (US size 15) needles and MC, cast on 33 sts. (The patt is worked over a multiple of 3 sts.)

1st patt row *K1, bring yarn to front between 2 needles then to back over RH needle to make an extra st—called *yarn over* or *yo*—, k2tog; rep from *. Rep last row 33 times more.

bind/cast off

Bind/cast off all 33 sts knitwise.

finishing touches

With right sides of the front and back together, join the seam along sides and bottom edge, beginning and ending the seam 4³/4in–5in/12–13cm from top. Turn right side out.

Handles (make 2)

Using two strands CC and 9mm (US size 13) double-pointed needles (dpn), cast on 4 sts.

1st row K4. (Do not turn knitting at end of row.)

2nd row With same side of knitting facing as last row, slide sts to other end of dpn, take yarn behind needle and pulling yarn tightly when working first st, knit to end.

Rep last row 29 times more or until tube measures desired length when stretched. Bind/cast off. Weave the handle in and out of the holes along the top edge of one side of the bag. Sew the ends of the tube together and move the seam inside the gathers of the bag to hide it. Attach the other handle in the same way.

lace-rib bag

The lace pattern for the Lace-rib Bag (shown above and below) creates a more open texture than the one used for the Lace String Bag on the previous page. The handles are worked in tube knitting with double-pointed needles.

ridged throw

A giant-needle knitting book wouldn't be complete without a pattern for a throw. This one might not be the fastest design to knit—it will take longer than a day—but it is far quicker than knitting something so big on ordinary-size needles. As a textural contrast on the throw, an off-white chunky chenille yarn is worked in garter stitch bands through the soft wool stockinette/stocking stitch. Equally, you can come up with your own ideas for textures. One that mixes a soft knitting wool (similar to the one used here) with a very few thin stripes in "rag" knitting running through it would look good.

here's how...

Choose whatever colors you like to knit this throw. If you choose white and off-white as here, be sure to wash your hands before you pick up your knitting—a tip I learned the hard way when crocheting white lace—and put it in a bag between times.

how big is it?
The finished throw measures 49¼in/125cm wide x 63in/160cm long.

which stitches?
- Stockinette/stocking stitch (St st)
- Garter stitch

how much yarn?
MC = chunky wool yarn in main color
  11 x 3½oz/100g balls Rowan *Polar*
  (white—shade no. 645—or chosen color)
CC = chunky chenille yarn in contrasting color
  4 x 3½oz/100g balls Rowan *Chunky Cotton Chenille*
  (off-white—shade no. 365—or chosen color)
(*See page 124 for yarn tips*)

which needles?
Long 15mm (US size 19) circular knitting needle

any extras?
¼yd/20cm of 44in/112cm wide printed or plain silk douppioni fabric, for tassels (optional)

what gauge/tension?
7½ sts and 10 rows to 4in/10cm measured over St st using two strands MC and 15mm (US size 19) needles.

before you start
- Using 15mm (US size 19) needles and two strands MC held tog, cast on 12 sts and work a swatch in St st to test your gauge/tension (see page 25). Knitting the throw to an exact size is not that important, but if your knitting is looser than recommended you may require more MC to work the number of rows specified.
- Make sure you have a long circular knitting needle. The knitting is worked back and forth in simple rows, but a pair of needles is too short to accommodate all the stitches comfortably.
- *For knitting abbreviations, turn to page 127.*

cast on
The throw is worked in St st stripes of MC and garter st stripes of CC, with a garter st border that has a slip-st edge.
Using 15mm (US size 19) circular needle and two strands CC held tog, cast on 94 sts using the double cast-on method (see page 18).
Knit back and forth in rows on circular needle as foll:
1st row Knit.
2nd row (WS) Insert needle into next st as if about to knit it but instead slip it from LH needle onto RH needle without knitting it—called *slip 1 knitwise* or *sl 1 knitwise*—, k to last st, sl last st knitwise.
3rd row (RS) P1, k to last st, p1.
4th row As 2nd row.
Break off CC. (4-row garter st border in CC is now complete.)
5th row (RS) Using two strands MC, p1, k to last st, p1.
6th row Using two strands MC, sl 1 knitwise, k2, p to last 3 sts, k2, sl 1 knitwise.
7th–20th rows Rep 5th–6th rows 7 times more.
Break off MC. (16-row St st stripe in MC is now complete.)
21st row Using two strands CC, p1, k to last st, p1.
22nd row Using two strands CC, sl 1 knitwise, k to last st, sl last st knitwise.

23rd–26th rows Rep 21st–22nd rows twice more. Break off CC. (6-row garter st stripe in CC is now complete.)

27th–30th rows Rep 5th–6th rows twice. Break off MC. (4-row St st stripe in MC is now complete.)

31st–36th rows Rep 21st–26th rows. Break off CC. (6-row garter st stripe in CC is now complete.)

Rep 5th–36th rows 3 times more.

Break off CC.

Rep 5th–20th rows once.

Break off MC. (16-row St st stripe in MC is now complete.)

Rep 21st–22nd rows twice. (4-row garter st border in CC is now complete.)

bind/cast off

Still using CC and with RS facing, bind/cast off loosely while purling first and last sts and knitting all other sts.

finishing touches

Weave in all loose ends.

Tassels

If desired, make a tassel for each of the four corners of the blanket (see page 122). For each tassel, cut six silk strips, each ³/4in/2cm by 14in/36cm, and line them up together. Tie a doubled strand of MC to a corner of the blanket, then use these yarn ends to tie around the center of the six strips. Fold the strips in half over the MC tying-knot, and use a separate silk strip to tie the strips together ³/4in/2cm below the tassel top (see page 122).

adding tassels

The Ridged Throw has a tassel tied to each of its four corners. Made with strips of patterned douppioni silk, the tassels (see above) provide an interesting detail and a contrasting texture to the soft wool throw ridged with bands of chenille (see below).

squares rag rug

Felt strips are so easy to knit with that even an absolute beginner can do it. This graphic rug is made in six simple garter-stitch-stripe squares, which are stitched together with the stripes perpendicular to each other to create a checkerboard effect. Pick your own color scheme so it goes with the room of your choice. If you want to economize, use real cotton "rag" strips instead of the felt and wool yarns used here. You'll find "rag" knitting a cinch to sew together because it is done with an ordinary sewing needle and strong thread, so it's easy to hide the stitches among the big rag loops.

here's how...

Be sure you read the tips in Before You Start. It is especially important to test the stretch on your felt lengthwise and widthwise before cutting the strips. Strips that are too stretchy will not have as much body and bounce.

how big is it?
The finished rug measures approximately 26in/66cm wide x 39in/99cm long.

which stitches?
Garter stitch

how much "yarn"?
A = gray felt
  3¹/2 yd/3.2m of 37in/94cm wide felt in dark gray or chosen color
B = chunky wool yarn to match felt
  3 x 3¹/2 oz/100g balls Rowan *Yorkshire Tweed Chunky* (dark green-gray—shade no. 550—or color to match chosen felt color)
C = chunky wool yarn in a contrasting color
  4 x 3¹/2 oz/100g balls Rowan *Polar* (mauve—shade no. 651—or chosen color)
(*See page 124 for yarn tips*)

try this!

- If you're making a rug with fabric strips rather than felt, cut them about 1¹/4in/3.5cm wide.

- For a bigger rug, just add on more rows of squares, or add on smaller squares around the outside edge to form a border.

which needles?
Pair of 15mm (US size 19) knitting needles

any extras?
- Strong sewing thread for sewing squares together
- Piece of gray felt (or baize) same size as finished rug for backing

what gauge/tension?
6¹/2 sts and 10¹/2 rows to 4in/10cm measured over garter st stripe patt using 15mm (US size 19) needles.

before you start
- Cut the felt strips ¹/2in/12mm wide or just slightly under this width (see next page for tips on cutting). The felt can be more stretchy either lengthwise or across the width, so cut the strips in the direction that has less stretch. Start by cutting a small ball of felt strips to use for testing your gauge/tension.
- Cast on 9 stitches and work a square of the garter stitch stripe patt using 15mm (US size 19) needles to check your stitch size. (See page 25 for more about gauge/tension.)
- The felt strips are worked together with a strand of chunky wool yarn—this makes the stitches stronger and gives the rug more body.
- *For knitting abbreviations, turn to page 127.*

cast on
The rug is made in 6 squares.
Striped square (make 6 alike)
Using 15mm (US size 19) needles and one strand each of A and B held tog, cast on 21 sts using the double cast-on method (the tail of yarn needed at

the front of the needle for this method should be about 51in/130cm long).

1st stripe row (WS) Still using one strand each of A and B, knit.

Drop A/B at side of work.

2nd stripe row (RS) Using 3 strands C, knit.

3rd stripe row As 2nd row.

Drop C at side of work.

**4th–7th rows Using A/B, knit.

Drop A/B at side of work.

8th–9th rows Using 3 strands C, knit.

Drop C at side of work.**

Rep from ** to ** 4 times more.

Break off C.

Using A/B, k 2 rows.

bind/cast off

Using A/B, bind/cast off all 21 sts loosely knitwise.

finishing touches

Arrange the squares in two rows of three squares, placing them so that the stripes in each square run perpendicular to those in the neighboring squares. (Make sure that the outside edge of the rug has neat edges without any loose yarn strands along them.) Using a sewing needle and thread, stitch the squares together edge to edge. Back the rug with a piece of gray felt cut to the same size as the rug, stitching it to the back around the edge.

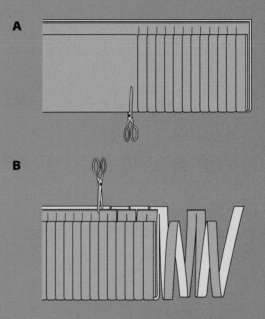

A

B

cut strips in a jiffy!

I usually tear my continuous "rag" strips for knitting, but some fabrics won't cooperate. Felt, for instance, can be torn but not in neat, even strips. If you are only cutting a few strips, you can cut back and forth as shown on page 60, but if you need to cut masses of strips, as for a rug, try this quick technique. Fold your fabric in half lengthwise, aligning the selvages. Then fold the fabric again lengthwise positioning the second fold about 2in/5cm from the selvages. Starting at the folded edge, cut the first strip from the fold toward the selvages, cutting through the second fold and ending the cut about $^3/_8$in/1cm from the selvages. Continue cutting strips in this way, leaving them all joined at the top (A). To create the continuous strip, clip through the bottom layer of fabric at the top of the first strip. When you unravel the first strip, you'll see where to clip through the fabric at the selvage to create the continuous strip (B).

colorwork
rag rug

"Rag" knitting with fat needles goes so quickly that a rug this size can be finished in a day by a fast knitter. This rug uses net and felt for the "rags." Like felt, net is a fabric that is a natural for giant-needle knitting. Its stretchiness allows it to slip comfortably along the needles and it's nice and bouncy underfoot. If you're looking for a bold palette similar to the one used for this rug, cotton felt and net are the perfect candidates. Craft felts come in vivid shades and synthetic net in equally bright ones. For a more tonal scheme, try stripes in brown, gray, black, and white.

here's how...

This rug is knitted using the simple colorwork technique called intarsia, but it could just as easily be worked in two pieces—each of them worked in simple stripes. Just stitch the two pieces together at the center when they're finished.

how big is it?
The finished rug measures 26in/66cm wide x 39¹/₂in/100cm long.

which stitches?
Garter stitch

how much "yarn"?
A = black felt
    3yd/2.8m of 37in/94cm wide felt in black or chosen main color
B = gold felt
    ³/₄yd/70cm of 37in/94cm wide felt in gold or chosen contrasting color
C = purple felt
    ³/₄yd/70cm of 37in/94cm wide felt in purple or chosen contrasting color
D = superchunky wool yarn to match felt in main color
    3 x 3¹/₂oz/100g balls Rowan *Big Wool* (black—shade no. 008—or shade to match chosen main color felt)
E = purple net
    2¹/₄yd/2m of 50in/127cm wide net in purple or chosen contrasting color
F = turquoise net
    2¹/₄yd/2m of 50in/127cm wide net in turquoise or chosen contrasting color
(*See page 124 for yarn tips*)

which needles?
Pair of 15mm (US size 19) knitting needles

preparing "yarns" for rag knitting
Make big balls of net and felt strips before you start your knitting. Follow the instructions on page 95 for preparing the fabric yarn really quickly. If you're making a rug with cotton fabric strips you can tear the strips instead of cutting them (see page 60).

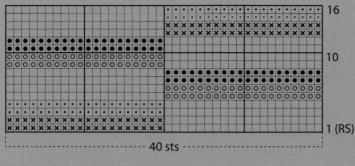

16

10

1 (RS)

40 sts

□ = A/D   ⊡ = B   ⊙ = C   ⊠ = E   ⊚ = F

try this!

This rug texture would make a great roomy tote bag—just cast on 20 stitches and follow half the chart for simple stripes. When the knitting reaches twice the desired length of the bag, fold it in half, join seams, line, and add a simple twisted-cord strap.

any extras?

Piece of black felt (or baize) same size as finished rug for backing, and matching sewing thread

what gauge/tension?

6 sts and 10½ rows to 4in/10cm measured over garter st colorwork patt using 15mm (US size 19) needles.

before you start

- Cut the felt strips ½in/12mm wide or just slightly under this width (see opposite page for tips on cutting). The felt can be more stretchy either across the width or lengthwise, so cut the strips in the direction that is less stretchy. Cut the net strips about 2¼in/5.5cm wide.
- Prepare a small ball of felt and net strips to use for testing your gauge/tension. It is not important to match recommended gauge/tension exactly if you are happy to have a rug of a slightly different size.
- When working from the colorwork chart, read RS (knit) rows from right to left and WS (knit) rows from left to right. Use a separate length of yarn for each block of color and twist yarns around each other on WS when changing colors to avoid holes (see page 79).
- For knitting abbreviations, turn to page 127.

cast on

Using 15mm (US size 19) needles and one strand each of A and D held tog, cast on 40 sts, using the double cast-on method (the tail of yarn needed at the front of the needle for this method should be about 2¾yd/2.5m long).

1st chart row (RS) K20 A/D, k20 E.
2nd chart row (WS) K20 E, k20 A/D.
3rd–4th chart rows As 1st–2nd rows.
Cont in this way in garter st foll chart until 16th chart row has been completed.
Rep 1st–16th chart rows 5 times more.
Rep 1st–8th chart rows. (104 rows worked from cast-on edge.)
Using A/D, k one row.

bind/cast off

Using A/D, bind/cast off all 40 sts loosely knitwise.

finishing touches

Weave in any loose ends on the wrong side of the rug. Back the rug with a piece of black felt cut to the same size as the rug, stitching it to the back around the edge.

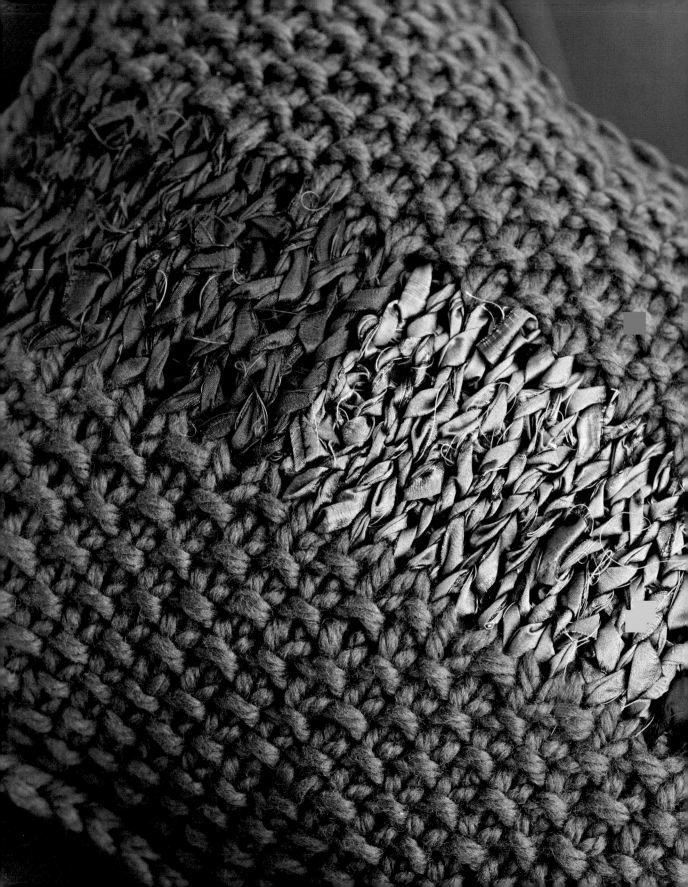

rag-stripe cushion

Silk-fabric knitting strips make a beautiful textural contrast with the wool yarn used for the seed/moss stitch pattern on this cushion cover. There's no need to prepare all your knitting strips before you start. I am sometimes so keen to begin my "rag" knitting that I only tear a couple of strips and let the fabric dangle at the end. When those strips are used up and the fabric is practically touching the knitting, I tear a couple more. The crisp "chain" edging around the pieces of this cushion cover is worked by picking up stitches with your knitting needle and fastening them off at the same time.

here's how...

The outside seam on the cushion cover is worked in double-sided backstitch with the wool yarn used for the seed/moss stitch. See page 120 for how to work this version of the backstitch.

how big is it?
The finished cushion measures 17³⁄₄in/45cm x 13³⁄₄in/35cm.

which stitches?
- Seed/moss stitch
- Stockinette/stocking stitch (St st)

how much "yarn"?
MC = superchunky wool yarn in main color
  3 x 3¹⁄₂oz/100g balls Rowan *Big Wool*
  (blue —shade no. 10—or chosen color)
A, B, and C = silk douppioni fabric in three contrasting colors
  ¹⁄₄yd/25cm of 44in/112cm wide silk douppioni in each of orange, blue-green, and mauve
(*See page 124 for yarn tips*)

any extras?
Pillow-form/cushion pad to fit

which needles?
Pair of 15mm (US size 19) knitting needles

what gauge/tension?
7 sts and 12 rows to 4in/10cm measured over seed/moss st using MC and 15mm (US size 19) needles.

before you start
- Cast on 10 stitches and work a square of seed/moss st using 15mm (US size 19) needles

and MC to check your stitch size. (See page 25 for more about gauge/tension.)
- Cut (or tear) your silk rag strips 1¹⁄₄in/3cm wide (see pages 60 and 95 for how to prepare strips).
- When working the blocks of color with the fabric strips, use a separate length of yarn for each block of color and twist yarns around each other on WS when changing colors to avoid holes (see page 79).
- *For knitting abbreviations, turn to page 127.*

cast on
The cushion is made in three pieces—a front with a rag stripe and two overlapping back pieces.
Front
Using 15mm (US size 19) needles and MC, cast on 32 sts loosely.
Beg seed/moss st patt as foll:
1st seed/moss st row (RS) *K1, p1; rep from * to end.
2nd seed/moss st row *P1, k1; rep from * to end.
Rep 1st–2nd rows to form seed/moss st patt.
Work 14 rows more in patt, so ending with a WS row.
Break off MC.
Using silk strips, beg rag stripe as foll:
Next row (RS) K11 A, k10 B, k11 C.
Next row P11 C, p10 B, p11 A.
Rep last 2 rows 3 times more, so ending with a WS row (8 rows in total have been worked in St st with rag yarn).
Cut off silk yarn.
Change back to MC and k one row.
Beg with a 2nd patt row, work 15 rows in seed/moss st.
Bind/cast off 31 sts loosely knitwise, leaving last loop on RH needle. Then to make a chain edging, pick up

and knit sts evenly all around rem 3 sides of front, binding/casting off sts as they are picked up.

Backs (make 2 alike)

Using 15mm (US size 19) needles and MC, cast on 20 sts loosely.

Work 42 rows in seed/moss st as for front, so ending with a WS row.

Bind/cast off 19 sts loosely knitwise, leaving last loop on RH needle, then cont around edge to make a chain edging as for front.

finishing touches

Pin the backs to the front with wrong sides facing, overlapping the backs at the center to form an envelope opening. Using MC and double-sided backstitch (see page 120) and stitching just inside the chain edging, sew the backs to the front so that the seam is on the outside forming a neat edging. Where three layers overlap, stitch the outside back layer to the front, then later stitch the inside back layer to the inside of the seams.

Insert the pillow-form/cushion pad.

choosing fabric-strip colors

The range of knitting yarn colors is more limited than the vast array of fabric colors you can get your hands on, so choose your yarn first then go in search of fabrics that will complement it. I pick douppioni silks because of the richness of their hues.

button cushion

This pattern is really great for a first project. Worked in garter stitch with a soft wool yarn, it has a button band of "rag" knitting. So you get to try "rag" knitting and learn how to make the very simplest of buttonholes as well. The type of silk fabric used for the knitting strips comes in such a range of stunning jewel colors that you will be spoiled for choice. Pick your silk color first, then the color for your knitting yarn. Any shade of silk will go well with a black or a white yarn—colors that are always available in chunky and superthick yarns.

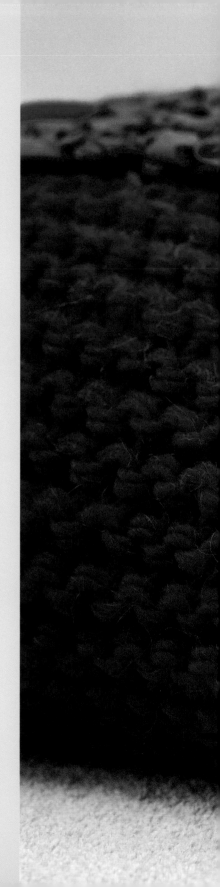

here's how...

Covered buttons were used for this cushion, but you can use any big buttons. Buttons you've been saving for a special occasion can become the starting point for your cushion—choose a yarn and fabric strips to complement them.

how big is it?
The finished cushion measures 17³/₄in/45cm square.

which stitches?
Garter stitch

how much "yarn"?
MC = chunky wool yarn in main color
    5 x 3¹/₂oz/100g balls Rowan *Polar*
    (brick red—shade no. 641—or chosen color)
A = silk douppioni fabric in contrasting color
    1yd/90cm of 44in/112cm wide silk douppioni in
    purple or chosen color
B = small amount of silk douppioni in
complementary tone for covering buttons

which needles?
Pair of 15mm (US size 19) knitting needles

any extras?
- 3 covered-button forms, 1¹/₂in/38mm in diameter
- Pillow-form/cushion pad to fit

what gauge/tension?
7¹/₂ sts and 13 rows to 4in/10cm measured over garter st using 15mm (US size 19) needles and silk rag strips or two strands of MC held tog.

before you start
- Cut (or tear) your silk rag strips 1¹/₂–1³/₄in/
    4–4.5cm wide (see pages 60 and 95 for how to

covering buttons
Kits for making covered buttons are widely available—each button consists of a metal top with teeth around the bottom edge for catching the fabric and a metal bottom with a button shank that snaps into the top over the raw fabric edges. They're very easy to make up.

prepare strips). Cut a small ball of rag strips to use for testing your gauge/tension and then adjust the width of the strips if necessary.

- Cast on 10 stitches and work a square of garter stitch using 15mm (US size 19) needles and two strands MC held together to check your stitch size. Do the same with the silk rag strips. (See page 25 for more about gauge/tension.)
- *For knitting abbreviations, turn to page 127.*

cast on

The cushion is made in three pieces—a back and two overlapping front pieces.

Back

Using 15mm (US size 19) needles and two strands MC held tog, cast on 34 sts.

Work in garter st (k every row) until back measures 17³⁄4in/45cm from cast-on edge—a total of 58 rows. Bind/cast off all 34 sts.

Front with buttonhole band

**Using 15mm (US size 19) needles and two strands MC held tog, cast on 34 sts.

Work in garter st (k every row) until front measures 9in/22.5cm from cast-on edge—a total of 29 rows.**
Break off MC.

Using A (rag strips), decrease 7 sts on next row as foll:

Next row (dec row) (RS) [K2, k2tog, k3, k2tog] 3 times, k2, k2tog, k3. (27 sts)

Work 2 rows more in garter st, so ending with a RS row.

Work buttonholes over next 2 rows as foll:

1st buttonhole row (WS) K6, *bind/cast off next st by knitting next 2 sts, inserting tip of LH needle through first st just knit and lifting it over the second st and off the RH needle (one st now on RH needle after buttonhole), k5; rep from * to end.

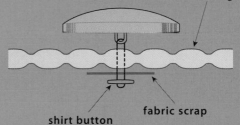

knitting

shirt button

fabric scrap

sew your buttons on securely!

Chunky, airy knitting doesn't make the best base for sewing on buttons. When I sewed the covered buttons to my Button Cushion, I remembered an old trick. You can give firmness to wobbly knitting by placing a scrap of fabric and a shirt button on the wrong side of the knitting under the main button shank. Just stitch through the shirt button, the fabric scrap, and the knitting each time your sewing thread catches in the main button.

2nd buttonhole row (RS) K across row, casting on one st over each st bound/cast off in last row (use single cast-on method—see page 17).

Work 3 rows more in garter st.

Bind/cast off all 27 sts knitwise.

Front without band

Work as for front with buttonhole band from ** to **.

Bind/cast off all 34 sts.

finishing touches

Pin the front with the buttonhole band to the back, with right sides together and cast-on edges aligned. Pin the other front to the back (it overlaps the buttonhole band). Using one strand of MC, sew the pieces together and weave in any loose ends. Turn right side out and insert the pillow-form/cushion pad. Cover buttons with B and sew in place.

black-and-white cushions

These eye-catching, bold, black-and-white cushion covers knit up really fast. Worked in soft chunky black cotton chenille yarn and a superthick white wool yarn, the contrasting yarn textures set each other off beautifully. Big giant-needle stitches make for comfortable cushion covers— they intensify the softness of the yarns. The covers slip on and off as easy as pie, the openings simply fastened with chunky twisted cords in contrasting colored yarns. Full instructions for making twisted cords are given on page 123.

here's how...

The white cushion with the black stripes (in the foreground on pages 108–109) is oblong in shape and the black cushion with white stripes (in the background on pages 108–109 and pictured on page 113) is square.

how big is it?
- **Oblong cushion:** The finished cushion measures 17³/₄in/45cm x 13³/₄in/35cm, excluding border.
- **Square cushion:** The finished cushion measures 17³/₄in/45cm square, excluding border.

which stitches?
- Stockinette/stocking stitch (St st)
- Garter stitch

how much yarn?
Oblong cushion

A = superchunky yarn
  2 x 3¹/₂oz/100g balls Rowan *Big Wool*
  (off-white—shade no. 01—or chosen color)
B = chunky chenille yarn
  1 x 3¹/₂oz/100g ball Rowan *Chunky Cotton Chenille*
  (black—shade no. 367—or chosen color)

Square cushion

A = superchunky yarn
  1 x 3¹/₂oz/100g ball Rowan *Big Wool*
  (off-white—shade no. 01—or chosen color)
B = chunky chenille yarn
  3 x 3¹/₂oz/100g balls Rowan *Chunky Cotton Chenille*
  (black—shade no. 367—or chosen color)
(*See page 124 for yarn tips*)

which needles?
15mm (US size 19) circular knitting needle

any extras?
- Small amounts of contrasting yarns for twisted cord fastenings
- Pillow-form/cushion pad to fit

what gauge/tension?
7–7¹/₂ sts and 10 rows to 4in/10cm measured over St st using one strand A and 15mm (US size 19) needles.

before you start
- To check your stitch size, cast on 10 sts and work a square of stockinette/stocking stitch using 15mm (US size 19) needles and one strand A. (See page 25 for more about how to check your gauge/tension.)
- Make sure you have a circular knitting needle. On both cushions, the knitting is worked back and forth in simple rows, but when working one-row stripes you need to slide the stitches back to the other end of the needle on every third row so you

try this!
- Don't worry about weaving in yarn ends on knitted cushion covers—they'll be hidden inside. Just knot loose ends together at the edges and clip them off close to the knot.

- If you find that the white pillow-form/ cushion pad shows through your knitting—big knitting makes the holes between stitches more obvious—make a simple matching slip cover for it using an inexpensive cotton fabric.

can work the following row on the same side. This allows you to carry the yarns neatly up the side of the knitting where possible and avoids lots of loose yarn ends at the edges.

- *For knitting abbreviations, turn to page 127.*

oblong cushion

cast on

The oblong cushion in the foreground on pages 108–109 is made in two pieces—a front and a back.

Front and back (both alike)

Using 15mm (US size 19) circular needle and one strand A, cast on 25 sts.

Beg with a k row, work 11in/28cm (about 28 rows) in St st, ending with a WS (purl) row.

Do not break off A, but drop it at side of work so it's ready to use again when needed.

Cont in St st for one-row stripes as foll:

1st stripe row (RS) Using two strands B held tog, knit.

*Keeping RS facing, slide sts back to other end of needle so you can pick up A and work another RS row as foll:

2nd stripe row (RS) Using one strand A, knit.

3rd stripe row (WS) Using two strands B, purl.

Keeping WS facing, slide sts back to other end of needle to work next row on WS row. (Cont using one strand A and two strands B throughout.)

4th stripe row (WS) Using A, purl.

5th stripe row (RS) Using B, knit.*

Rep from * to * twice more.

Rep 2nd and 3rd rows once more, so ending with a WS row in B.

Cut off A and cont with B only.

Work 5 rows in garter st (k every row) for border, so ending with a RS row.

oblong cushion—alternative colorways

You can ring the changes on the Oblong Cushion by using different colorways or textures, or varying the width of the stripes. For example, spread the narrow black stripes farther apart and add in a random stripe in a different color (see above). Alternatively, knit the cushion cover in black and use a superthick multicolored yarn for the narrow one-row stripes (see below).

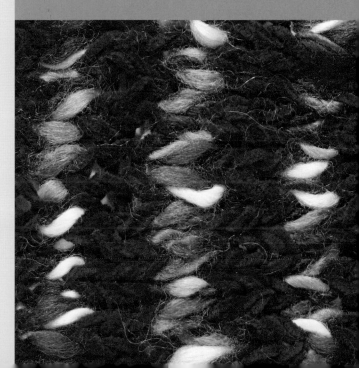

bind/cast off

Still using B and with WS facing, bind/cast off all 25 sts knitwise.

finishing touches

Do not press the knitting.

With right sides facing, sew the back and front together around three sides, matching the stripes and leaving the garter stitch end open.

Turn right side out.

Tie fastenings

Make three chunky twisted-cord ties each 12in/30cm long, using six strands of medium-weight contrasting yarn held together (see page 123 for how to make twisted cords). If desired, use two or three colors in the cords. Knot both ends of the cords.

Insert the pillow-form/cushion pad, then, at equal intervals, poke the cords through the two layers of the opening next to the garter stitch border and tie.

square cushion

cast on

The Square Cushion on the next page is made in two pieces—a back and a front.

Front and back (both alike)

Using 15mm (US size 19) circular needle and two strands B held tog, cast on 33 sts.

Using two strands B and one strand A throughout, cont as foll:

1st row (RS) Using B, knit.

2nd row Using B, purl.

3rd row Using B, knit.

4th and 5th rows As 2nd and 3rd rows.

Do not break off B, but drop it at side of work so it's ready to use again when needed.

6th row (WS) Using A, knit to create a ridge on RS. Cut off A.

Keeping WS facing, slide sts back to other end of needle so you can pick up B and work another WS row as foll:

7th row (WS) Using B, knit.

8th row (RS) Using B, knit.

9th row (WS) Using B, purl.

10th row (RS) Using B, knit.

11th and 12th rows As 9th and 10th rows.

Rep 6th–12th rows 5 times more, so there are a total of 6 white stripe bands.

Work 4 rows garter st (k every row) for border, so ending with a RS row.

bind/cast off

Still using B and with WS facing, bind/cast off all 33 sts knitwise.

finishing touches

Follow the Finishing Touches for the Oblong Cushion (see left), but make four twisted-cord ties instead of three.

square cushion—alternative colorways

The Square Cushion above with its black background and narrow white ridged stripes would look good paired with one worked with a white background and narrow black stripes (see left). To add a bit of color to the finished knitting, thread a length of superthick variegated yarn on a yarn needle and weave it in and out of the stitches down the center of the contrasting stripes.

variegated yarn cushion

Devoted knitters love yarn and collect masses of it. Only one side of this stockinette/stocking stitch cushion cover is knitted, so you can splash out and buy a more expensive yarn than usual. Keep in mind that all good knitting designs start with the yarns and buying beautiful, good-quality ones is worth it. They make the experience of knitting a joy. There's more to any yarn than looks. Be sure to feel your yarn before you buy it—knitting is as much a tactile experience as a visual one.

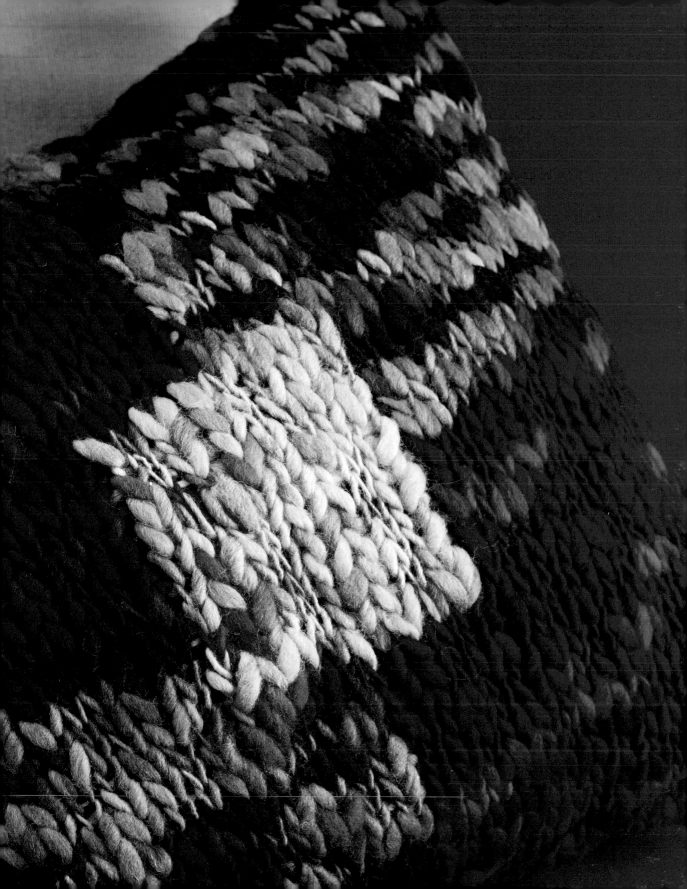

here's how...

Follow the chart to knit this cushion cover. If you want to change the shapes of the blocks of color, trace the outline of the chart on a piece of graph paper and chart your own creation to knit to.

how big is it?
The finished cushion measures 16³/₄in/42cm square.

which stitches?
Stockinette/stocking stitch (St st)

how much yarn?
A = variegated chunky wool yarn in first contrasting color
   1 x 3¹/₂oz/100g hank Colinette *Point 5*
   (shade no. 48 or chosen color)
B = variegated chunky wool yarn in second contrasting color
   1 x 3¹/₂oz/100g hank Colinette *Point 5*
   (shade no. 122 or chosen color)
C = variegated chunky wool yarn in third contrasting color
   1 x 3¹/₂oz/100g hank Colinette *Point 5*
   (shade no. 18 or chosen color)
   (*See page 124 for yarn tips*)

which needles?
Pair of 12mm (US size 17) knitting needles

any extras?
- A complementary cotton fabric for the cushion cover—one piece 17³/₄in/45cm square for the front, and two pieces each 17³/₄in/45cm by 11in/31cm for the overlapping backs
- Sewing thread for stitching on knitted front and sewing cushion cover
- Pillow-form/cushion pad to fit

what gauge/tension?
7¹/₂ sts and 10¹/₂ rows to 4in/10cm measured over St st using 12mm (US size 17) needles.

before you start
- To check your stitch size, cast on 10 stitches and work a square of St st using 12mm (US size 17) needles.

variegated yarn choices
Select three yarn colors of similar lightness or darkness for this cushion so they don't contrast too starkly. Variegated yarn colorings further blur the distinction between the three yarns, softening the geometric colorwork shapes.

- It is not important to match exactly the recommended gauge/tension if you are happy to have a cushion of a slightly different size.
- When working from the colorwork chart, read RS (knit) rows from right to left and WS (purl) rows from left to right. Use a separate length of yarn for each block of color and twist yarns around each other on WS when changing colors to avoid holes (see page 79).
- For knitting abbreviations, turn to page 127.

cast on

The knitting is for the front of the cushion only and is stitched to the front of a fabric cushion cover.
Using 12mm (US size 17) needles, A, and the double cast-on method (see page 18), cast on 16 sts; then using B, cast on 16 sts more. (32 sts)
1st chart row (RS) K16 B, k16 A.
2nd chart row (WS) P16 A, p16 B.
Cont in this way in St st foll chart until 44th chart row has been completed.

bind/cast off

Using A and B, bind/cast off all 32 sts loosely knitwise.

finishing touches

Weave in any loose ends on the wrong side.
Pin the knitted piece out to the correct size right side down on a padded surface and gently press on the wrong side using a damp cloth and a warm iron.
To make the fabric cover, pin one long side of each back piece to the sides of the front piece and sew the seams with a 1/2in/1.5cm seam allowance. Turn under and stitch 1/2in/1.5cm hems along the outer edges of the backs (the edges that will be along the opening). Then fold the backs onto the front with right sides

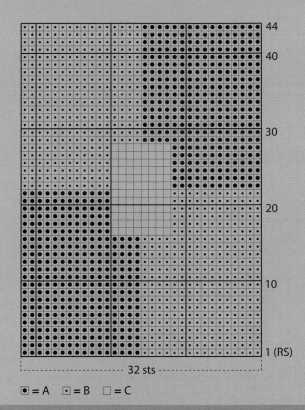

⊡ = A   ⊡ = B   □ = C

try this!

Don't worry if your knitting isn't coming out exactly the right size. Pressing the finished piece will ease it into shape. To be sure of a good fit, buy your pillow-form/cushion pad after pressing the knitting. You can adjust the sizes of the pieces for the fabric cushion cover to match the knitting, too.

together and stitch the remaining seams around the edge. Turn right side out and press.
Using sewing thread, stitch the knitting to the front of the fabric cover so that the edges meet the seamlines and hide them.
Insert the pillow-form/cushion pad.

useful things to know

seams and linings...

seams for giant-needle knits

Stitching seams on giant knits needs to be done quite carefully for a good finish. Any flaws in seams are more obvious than on smaller-scale knitted textures. The best method to use is a simple overcast stitch. For seams that show on the outside, double-sided backstitch makes a neat finishing touch (see Rag-stripe Cushion on page 100 and Tweed Handbag on page 72). Rag knitting should be stitched together either with a shallow overcast stitch, or edge-to-edge with a slip stitch and using a sewing needle and a strong sewing thread.

To weave in loose ends on giant-needle knits, use a blunt-ended needle and weave into the stitches invisibly on the wrong side. Split really thick yarns into two strands and weave in each strand separately. Clip off the woven-in ends close to the knitting. If the knitting has a wrong side that will not show, such as inside a cushion cover, you can knot together the loose ends, instead of weaving them in, and clip off close to the knot.

Working an overcast seam

Work the overcast stitches close to the edge of the two pieces of knitting. Use a blunt-ended yarn needle and matching yarn if the piece has been knitted with yarn, and a sewing needle and thread if it has been knitted with fabric strips.

Place the two pieces with right sides together and edges aligned. Pin if necessary. Take a couple of stitches in the same place to start, then work stitches at equal intervals as shown top right. Secure with a couple of stitches.

Working a double-sided backstitch seam

This stitch looks like backstitch on both sides of the work, so it is perfect for decorative, outside seams.

Every other stitch on each side of the seam is double, but this will not be obvious on the finished seam since the second stitch completely covers the first stitch under it.

Make the first stitch on the underside and work a stitch backward on the other side of the knitting to match it, then make a stitch over the first stitch as shown by the arrow (A). Continue working the stitches as shown in the following illustrations (B and C). Repeat steps A, B, and C along the seam (working two stitches forward, then one stitch backward).

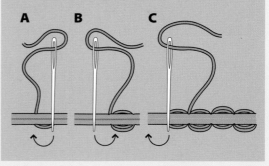

OVERCAST SEAM

DOUBLE-SIDED BACKSTITCH

A   B   C

linings for giant-needle knits

Bags and totes that will get a lot of use are much more practical if they have a fabric lining. Linings are also helpful for cushion covers knitted with giant needles, since the white pillow-form/cushion pad inside can show through the large textures. These linings are simply slipped on over the bare pillow-form/cushion pad before the knit cover is put on.

If the lining fabric will show through the knitting at all, make sure that it matches the main yarn used. If the lining won't show through—for instance, inside a closely knit bag or tote—you can choose a complementary color or print.

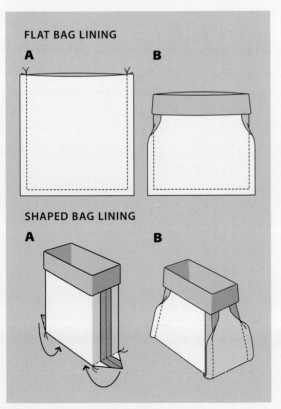

FLAT BAG LINING

A   B

SHAPED BAG LINING

A   B

Lining a simple flat bag

A bag made of two squares or rectangles is really easy to line. Use the knitted front of your bag to calculate the size of the two bag lining pieces. Add extra for the 1/2 in/1.5cm seam allowances and about 1 1/2 in/4cm at the top for a hem. Buy an easy-to-stitch cotton fabric.

Cut two pieces of fabric to the correct size and place them with right sides together. Stitch 1/2 in/1.5cm from the edge around the two sides and bottom, leaving the top open (A, top left). Press the top of the side seams open, then fold down the top hem and press (B, top left). Insert the lining and stitch it invisibly to the bag along the hem fold.

Lining a shaped bag

Lining a shaped bag is a little more difficult, but the principle is the same. Use the bag pieces as the guide for cutting the lining. Allow for 1/2 in/1.5cm seam allowances and for a 1 1/2 in/4cm hem at the top. If desired you can press an iron-on interfacing onto the fabric pieces before stitching them together.

Lining A (bottom far left) is the type of lining used for the Rag Shoulder Bag on page 58 and lining B next to it is the type used for the Tweed Handbag on page 72. The corners of bag lining A are pinched together and stitched across to form a triangle as shown—the triangle points are then folded onto the bottom of the bag shape as shown by the arrows to make a simple box shape. Bag lining B is made of three pieces—a shaped gusset for the base and sides, a front piece, and a back piece. When the linings are ready, insert them in the bag and stitch to the inside of the bag along the hem fold.

trims for giant-needle knits...

decorative add-ons

Giant-needle knits look great with added decorative trims, handmade or readymade. There are countless pretty add-ons available these days—tassels, fringe, ribbons, pompoms, braids, beads, and sequins. All you need to do is stitch them to your finished scarf, bag, cushion, or throw. The knitting process will be so much more enjoyable if you know you are making them to show off a treasured trim. You might even want to design the knitting to suit the trim, rather than the other way around.

The pompoms, beads, tassels, and fringe I've used on my knits are just examples of how you can decorate and personalize your own knitting.

Making your own trims is more satisfying than buying them. If you're new to knitting, you may not know how to make the three simple trims that seasoned knitters often use. There are instructions for how to make quick pompoms on page 57 and directions here for how to make tassels and a fringe. You can make tassels and fringe from any yarn you like, a mixture of yarns, or even ribbon, strung beads, or fabric strips. Tassels and fringe both make good trims for throws, scarves, cushions, and bags.

Although your giant-needle knitting is done in a flash, take your time with handmade trims. Never rush finishing touches. Perfect, carefully finished trims will add that extra professional touch that makes your handknit a real eyecatcher.

Making a tassel

To make a tassel, first cut lots of strands of yarn, a little longer than twice the desired length of the tassel. Hold the strands together and tie a separate length of yarn tightly around the center (A). (Leave the ends of the tying yarn long to use for fastening to your knitting.) Fold the tassel strands in half at the

tie and wrap another length of yarn around them to form a "ball" of strands at the top and secure (B).

Making fringe

To make fringe, first cut a length of yarn at least 1in/2.5cm longer than the desired length of the finished fringe and fold it in half. (For a plumper fringe, you can use two or more strands together.) Insert a crochet hook from back to front through the edge of the knitting and draw the yarn through. Then draw the ends of the yarn through the loop (A) and pull to tighten. Work the fringe as close together or far apart as desired (B). When the fringe is complete, trim the ends to even them.

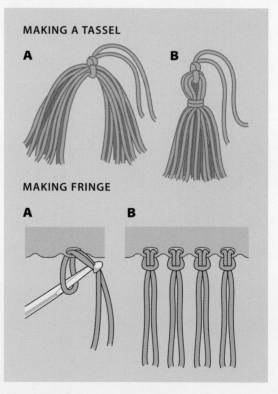

MAKING A TASSEL

A   B

MAKING FRINGE

A   B

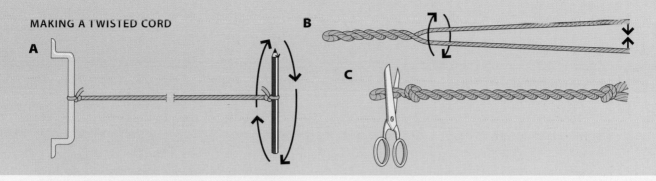

A

B

C

decorative fastenings and straps

The fastenings you use on bags and cushions, and the straps and handles for bags, are important, eyecatching finishing touches. When creating your own giant-needle projects, focus a lot of attention on what you pick for these. Fastenings for bags can be buttons, buckles, or drawstrings; for cushions: buttons and cord ties. Avoid zippers to keep the techniques as simple as possible.

As for the straps and handles on my bag designs, there are wooden handles and knitted tube handles (String Bags on pages 82–87), a braid strap (Rag Shoulder Bag on page 58), a garter-stitch handle (Tweed Handbag on page 72), fabric handles (Rag Shopping Bag on page 68), and cord straps (Drawstring Knapsacks and Star-stitch Bag on pages 76 and 64). Hopefully, you'll think of even more decorative fastenings, straps, and handles for your own designs. This would be an opportunity to introduce simple crochet into your knits. Or search craft stores and fabric stores for enticing readymade cords, ribbons, and braids for handbag straps and handles. Ever wondered what you could use those delectable, unique huge buttons found in flea markets for—giant-needle handbags and totes, and cushions, of course! Often on giant-needle textures there's no need for buttonholes either—the buttons will pass right through the knitting.

Twisted cords feature a lot in my designs, so there are instructions for how to make them yourself on

this page. A single yarn or a mixture of yarns can be used to make them. Or you can introduce a fabric strip or thin ribbon for an unusual effect. For clarity, only a single strand is shown in the instructions, but for thick cords you will need to start out with at least two strands. There is no hard and fast rule about how long to cut the strands for a specific length of twisted cord, as it depends on how stretchy the yarn is and on how tightly the cord is twisted. You will, however, need strands that are at least twice the length of the finished cord since they are folded in half to form the twist. For all the twisted cords used for the projects in this book, I have indicated how many strands of yarn to use and how long to cut them.

Making a twisted cord

Cut the number of strands required, to the length specified. Then tie one end of the group of strands to a stationary object—I use a door handle. Tie the other end to a pencil. Near the pencil, hold the yarn loosely in one hand and with the other hand turn the pencil round and round (A). Keep the yarn taut as you twist it. Once the yarn starts to kink, fold it in half, still keeping it taut. Let one half of the yarn twist around the other half, releasing it gradually (B). Cut the ends of the yarn from the door handle and pencil and knot them together. Tie a knot at the folded end as well and trim off the ends (C).

buying yarn...

Yarn manufacturers change their yarn colors fairly often, so it is almost impossible to guarantee that every shade in the book will still be available when you knit the projects. The shade numbers used are given in the instructions, but feel free to use your own choice of colors.

When possible, try to use the specific brand and type of yarn recommended in the pattern (see page 126 for addresses).

However, if you need to use a substitute yarn, figure out first how many yards/meters you need rather than relying on the weights. The specifications for the yarns used in this book are listed here. The recommended gauge/tension and needle size, and the actual-size photos of the yarns, will help you find a yarn of a similar thickness.

Rowan yarns used in this book

All Seasons Cotton
- A medium-weight cotton yarn; 60% cotton, 40% acrylic/microfiber
- 1³/₄oz/50g (approximately 98yd/90m) per ball
- Recommended gauge/tension: 16–18 sts and 23–25 rows to 4in/10cm over St st using 4¹/₂–5¹/₂mm (US size 7–9) knitting needles

Biggy Print
- A superchunky wool yarn; 100% merino wool
- 3¹/₂oz/100g (approximately 33yd/30m) per ball
- Recommended gauge/tension: 5¹/₂ sts and 7 rows to 4in/10cm over St st using 20mm (US size 35) knitting needles

Big Wool
- A superchunky wool yarn; 100% merino wool
- 3¹/₂oz/100g (approximately 87yd/80m) per ball
- Recommended gauge/tension: 7¹/₂–8 sts and 10–12 rows to 4in/10cm over St st using 12mm or 15mm (US size 17 or 19) knitting needles

Chunky Cotton Chenille
- A chunky cotton chenille yarn; 100% cotton
- 3¹/₂oz/100g (approximately 153yd/140m) per ball
- Recommended gauge/tension: 16–18 sts and 21–25 rows to 4in/10cm over St st using 4¹/₂–5mm (US size 7–8) knitting needles

Cotton Tape
- A tubular tape yarn; 100% cotton
- 1³/₄oz/50g (approximately 71yd/65m) per ball
- Recommended gauge/tension: 13–14 sts and 17–19 rows to 4in/10cm over St st using 8mm (US size 11) knitting needles

Kid Silk Haze
- A fine mohair yarn; 70% super kid mohair and 30% silk
- 1oz/25g (approximately 229yd/210m) per ball
- Recommended gauge/tension: 18–25 sts and 23–34 rows to 4in/10cm over St st using 3¹/₄–5mm (US size 3–8) knitting needles

Linen Print
- A tubular tape yarn; 70% viscose and 30% linen
- 1³/₄oz/50g (approximately 60yd/55m) per ball
- Recommended gauge/tension: 13 sts and 16 rows to 4in/10cm over St st using 8mm (US size 11) knitting needles

Lurex Shimmer
- A fine metallic yarn; 80% viscose and 20% polyester
- 1oz/25g (approximately 104yd/95m) per ball
- Recommended gauge/tension: 29 sts and 41 rows to 4in/10cm over St st using 3¹/₂mm (US size 3) knitting needles

Polar
- A chunky wool yarn; 60% pure new wool, 30% alpaca and 10% acrylic

- 3½ oz/100g (approximately 109yd/100m) per ball
- Recommended gauge/tension: 12 sts and 16 rows to 4in/10cm over St st using 8mm (US size 11) knitting needles

Summer Tweed

- A lightweight silk and cotton blend yarn; 70% silk and 30% cotton
- 1¾oz/50g (approximately 118yd/108m) per hank
- Recommended gauge/tension: 16 sts and 23 rows to 4in/10cm over St st using 5mm (US size 8) knitting needles

Yorkshire Tweed Chunky

- A chunky wool yarn; 100% pure new wool
- 1¾oz/50g (approximately 71yd/65m) per ball
- Recommended gauge/tension: 12 sts and 16 rows to 4in/10cm over St st using 8mm (US size 11) knitting needles

Colinette yarns used in this book

Point 5

- A chunky variegated yarn; 100% pure wool
- 3½oz/100g (approximately 54yd/50m) per hank
- Recommended gauge/tension: 7½ sts and 9 rows to 4in/10cm over St st using 12mm (US size 17) knitting needles

Tagliatelli

- A tape yarn; 90% merino pure wool and 10% nylon
- 3½oz/100g (approximately 158yd/145m) per hank
- Recommended gauge/tension: 11 sts and 15 rows to 4in/10cm over St st using 8mm (US size 11) knitting needles

Rowan *All Seasons Cotton*

Rowan *Biggy Print*

Rowan *Big Wool*

Rowan *Chunky Cotton Chenille*

Rowan *Cotton Tape*

Rowan *Kid Silk Haze*

Rowan *Linen Print*

Rowan *Lurex Shimmer*

Rowan *Polar*

Rowan *Summer Tweed*

Rowan *Yorkshire Tweed Chunky*

Colinette *Point 5*

Colinette *Tagliatelli*

addresses...

addresses for giant needles

I am grateful to Lion Brand Yarns in New York for sending me the colored knitting needles pictured on page 11. These are must-haves if, like me, you can't stand seeing another gray needle in your knitting-needle jar or in your needle-clicking hands.

To get these needles, as well as masses of economic and colorful yarns and more (including a fantastic "fur" yarn), contact Lion Brand at their website: www.lionbrandyarn.com

for more information

Ask for a free catalog:
C&T Publishing, Inc.
P.O. Box 1456
Lafayette, CA 94549
800-284-1114
email: ctinfo@ctpub.com
website: www.ctpub.com

addresses for buying yarns

To find out where to buy Rowan or Colinette yarns (see pages 124 and 125) near you, contact their websites:
www.knitrowan.com
www.colinette.com

For quilting or fabric knitting supplies:
Cotton Patch Mail Order
3404 Hall Lane
Dept. CTB
Lafayette, CA 94549
800-835-4418
925-283-7883
email: quiltusa@yahoo.com
website: www.quiltusa.com

Note: Fabric and yarn used in the items featured may not currently be available because manufacturers keep most products in print for only a short time.

author's acknowledgments...

I couldn't have asked for a better team for the making of this book! They have all been a pleasure to work with. Thanks to Anne Wilson for her wonderful design, to Kate Simunek for her artistic expertise, and to John Heseltine for so sensitively photographing everything. Thanks also to Anna Sanderson and Auberon Hedgecoe at Mitchell Beazley for all their help and patience, to Kate Buller and Ann Hinchcliffe at Rowan for supplying me with the fabulous Rowan yarns so quickly whenever I asked, and to Marilyn Wilson for her meticulous knitting-pattern checking.

My gratitude, as ever, goes to my good friend Nancy Thomas for keeping me up-to-date with the goings-on in the knitting world in the United States and for continually sharing her "passion for knitting" with me.

And as far as this book goes, thanks most of all to Susan Berry for getting the whole project moving, for art directing my knitting design work, for coming up with many of the best ideas for the book in terms of its allover look as well as content, and for giving me just the encouragement I needed.

knitting abbreviations...

To make knitting instructions easier to follow, they are written with the use of abbreviations. The abbreviations used in this book are very logical and quick to learn:

beg	begin(ning)
CC	contrasting color
cm	centimeter(s)
cont	continu(e)(ing)
dec	decreas(e)(ing)
dpn	double-pointed needle(s)
foll	follow(s)(ing)
g	gram(s)
in	inch(es)
inc	increas(e)(ing)
k	knit
k2tog	knit two stitches together
LH needle	left-hand needle
m	meter(s)
MC	main color
mm	millimeter(s)
oz	ounce(s)
p	purl
patt	pattern
psso	pass slipped stitch over
rem	remain(s)(ing)
rep	repeat(s)(ing)
RH needle	right-hand needle
RS	right side(s)
sl	slip a stitch from LH to RH needle without knitting it
sl 1 knitwise	insert RH needle into next st on LH needle as if about to knit it and slip it from the left-hand to right-hand needle without knitting it
ssk	slip 1 knitwise, slip 1 knitwise, insert tip of left needle into fronts of 2 slipped sts and k2tog
st(s)	stitch(es)
St st	stockinette/stocking stitch
tog	together
WS	wrong side(s)
yd	yard(s)
yo	yarn over RH needle to make extra stitch

* Repeat instructions after asterisk or between asterisks as many times as instructed.
[ ] Repeat instructions inside square brackets as many times as instructed.

English-language terminology...
Most terms used in US and UK knitting patterns are the same, but a few are different. Where terms are different, they appear in the instructions divided by a /.

US	UK
bind off	cast off
seed stitch	moss stitch
stockinette stitch	stocking stitch
gauge	tension (size of stitch)
yarn over (yo)	yarn forward (yf, yfwd), yarn over needle (yon), or yarn round needle (yrn)

knitting needle sizes...
This chart shows you how the different knitting needle size systems compare.

US sizes	UK metric
000	1 1/2mm
00	
0	2mm
1	2 1/4mm
	2 1/2mm
2	2 3/4mm
	3mm
3	3 1/4mm
4	3 1/2mm
5	3 3/4mm
	4mm
6	
7	4 1/2mm
8	5mm
9	5 1/2mm
10	6mm
10 1/2	6 1/2mm
	7mm
	7 1/2mm
11	8mm
13	9mm
15	10mm
17	12mm
19	15mm
35 (19mm)	20mm
50	25mm

index...